ASTROLOGY FOR HAPPINESS AND SUCCESS

D0061851

ASTROLOGY FOR HAPPINESS AND SUCCESS

MECCA WOODS

FROM ARIES TO PISCES, CREATE THE LIFE YOU WANT— BASED ON YOUR ASTROLOGICAL SIGN!

Adams Media
New York   London   Toronto   Sydney   New Delhi

 **adams**media

Adams Media
An Imprint of Simon & Schuster, Inc.
57 Littlefield Street
Avon, Massachusetts 02322

First Adams Media trade paperback edition October 2018

Interior design by Heather McKiel
Interior illustrations by Emma Taylor

Manufactured in the United States of America

10 9 8 7 6 5 4 3 2 1

Library of Congress Cataloging-in-Publication Data has been applied for.

ISBN 978-1-5072-0782-6
ISBN 978-1-5072-0783-3 (ebook)

CONTENTS

ACKNOWLEDGMENTS

I'd like to take this moment to express my heartfelt gratitude for all of the people who helped me to make this book, my first book, possible. Those people include: the team at Adams Media, especially my editors Julia Jacques and Sarah Doughty for their patience, guidance, and wholehearted support of this book; my brilliant and supportive literary agent, Danielle Chiotti—this wild Sagittarius thanks you for your cool-headed Virgo magic; astrology extraordinaires Rebecca Gordon, Jason Fleming, and Janelle Belgrave for your wisdom, support, and friendship; the healers, diviners, and witches that I've met along the way; and my family—Celeste, Howard, Lois, Yabbee, and Suraiyah—for their cheerleading and love. A big thank you also goes out to my readers and the folks that have been following my work since the early days—thanks for sticking with me.

INTRODUCTION

For as long as astrology has been around (more than two thousand years, to be exact!), astrologers have used it as a tool to help bring about a desired result or outcome using both cosmic timing and the power of the stars that a person is born under—a.k.a. the zodiac sign. Fast forward to today and we find the field of astrology experiencing a renaissance, being used for all sorts of things, from picking the perfect date to picking the perfect outfit. Astrology helps us to better identify our special qualities and teaches us how to marry them with auspicious timing to find the things in life that we're searching for. And if astrology can help us with the smaller stuff, why wouldn't we use its power to help us find the happiness and success that we're *really* looking for?

You don't have to be an astrology expert to get the most out of this book. What you'll find in the chapters to come is easy-to-follow astrological advice that can be applied to your life in the real world. In the love sections, you'll learn how your sign can improve your relationships with family and friends and how to get over a heart-break. In the career sections, you'll learn what kinds of jobs and workplace environments are best suited for your sign and how to better achieve your goals. Last but not least, in the wellness sections, you'll learn what to do when you're feeling off-balance and want to feel like yourself again, along with how to turn your home space into a sanctuary.

Happiness and success are within your reach. Look to the stars to find them!

CHAPTER 1
ARIES: MARCH 21–APRIL 19

Fueled by passion, courage, and an unquenchable thirst for life, you're a natural-born leader who lets very little get in the way of what you want. And if there's one thing you want, it's to live your life free of hesitation or following someone else's rules. Being an Aries, it's important to you to maintain your sense of independence and adventure, as without it you can easily feel depleted.

In this chapter, you'll find tips for bouncing back during those times when you feel like you've lost your spark, as well as how to take the spark you do have and magnify it in a way that can help you to make things that you want to happen, happen—from love and career success to overall well-being. When you walk away from this chapter and put the information in it to use, you will begin to feel like the warrior you are.

FIRE IT UP

Known as the firstborn of the zodiac and a fire sign, you're a true pioneer and innovator—often inspiring the rest of us to go after the things we're passionate about with the same zest and fearlessness that you bring to your everyday life. Because of the sheer determination and the fire that you carry in your heart, there's hardly anything that can stop you from going after something (or someone) you want. One reason for this is because your zodiac sign is ruled by Mars, the planet associated with the Roman god of war. It's with your warrior spirit that you're able to conquer challenges set before you, all the while venturing out into new territories and experiences without any of the fears or reservations that may slow others down. As an Aries, you are motivated by the need to live life fast, free, and unfettered. While some may criticize your approach as being reckless and impulsive, at your core you have a deep-seated need to express yourself as authentically and sincerely as possible. In fact, originality is one of your superpowers—as is your way of bluntly telling it like it is. These are just some of the things about you that make you a force to be reckoned with.

However, for all of the natural, unbridled power that you possess, it can be all too easy to burn yourself out when you allow the fear of losing or appearing weak to get the best of you. As the zodiac sign linked with the fearless god who wins at all costs and never backs down from a fight, it's important for you to recognize that not everything you do has to be a battle or a win-lose scenario.

Acknowledging this takes self-awareness, and part of this awareness means having the ability to make room for others to win—recognizing that their winning doesn't mean that you lose. For one thing, the idea of losing is rooted in scarcity—that there's not enough to go around. But how can you really lose in a world that has so much to give? Another element of self-awareness means knowing when you're being motivated by external rewards, like the awe or approval of others or instant gratification instead of something intrinsic, like creativity or passion. Allowing insecurity to take the front seat means making decisions that may not be thought all the way through, succumbing to anger when things don't go your way, and refusing to show vulnerability or take responsibility for your actions. Meanwhile, when passion and creativity are your source of motivation—pieces of you that exist beyond the borders of external reward and scarcity—you give yourself the freedom to truly *be* yourself.

And since we're talking about passion, it doesn't take much for you to set hearts ablaze. When an Aries is in love, it's hot, hot, hot!

YOUR APPROACH TO LOVE

Bold, daring, and passionate, you are truly on fire when it comes to love and romance. Seeking independence, you attract love interests through your thirst for adventure, tough talk, and can-do attitude. When you're into someone, it won't be hard for them to tell, as you prefer being direct about what you want rather than playing shy. You also prefer partners who do the same. If a significant other can't match you toe to toe with the same passion, fun, and energy that you bring to the table, you'll lose interest fast. The brave soul who can keep your attention long enough for you to stick around will be able to hold their own, especially when it comes to an argument. After all, an argument is like an aphrodisiac to an Aries. Just think of all the make-up sex there is to be had.

You've got the kind of confidence that makes you hard to resist, but there's nothing like having a few weapons—I mean, *tools*—in your arsenal to add to your allure. The following are a few essentials for your toolkit.

WOWING WITH COLOR

Although you rarely play shy, adding just the right colors to your wardrobe can help you catch the eye of that special someone without you even having to make a move. Not only can color be used to ramp up your sex appeal, it can also be incorporated into your wardrobe when you need a little pick-me-up. Here are the go-to colors for when you're ready to turn up the heat.

Red

As far as astrology and colors go, this *is* your color, Aries. Hot and fiery—red is the go-to color when it comes to getting the heart racing and the blood pumping. Wearing this signature color won't only make you feel like you can conquer anything or anyone in front of you but also make you feel irresistible, as your admirers won't be able to keep their eyes off you.

Bright Orange

A warm, eye-catching color in the red family, bright orange is associated with enthusiasm, joy, and magnetism. Wearing this color or having it in a place where you can see it regularly can stimulate joy and confidence within you, which will pull others to you like a magnet.

Hot Pink

While soft pinks have long been linked with the more romantic side of love, hot pink incorporates vibrancy, warmth, and a sense of fun. You can add this color to your ensemble when you want to bring out your more playful side—the glow of someone having fun is *hella* attractive.

SCENTS FOR POWER AND SEDUCTION

With these key power colors, you'll be making a statement and drawing in admirers without saying a word! And while you are at it, there are also a few scents to consider before you head out on that next hot date...

Because of your fiery, ambitious spirit you need fragrances that stand out and pack a punch—just like you. Look to fragrances or essential oils that are comprised of spicy, musky, or herbal notes. The following are a few essential scents to complement your spunky personality and passionate soul.

Spicy

Scents that fall under the spicy category are distinct and inherently powerful. They're great when it comes to waking up the senses, turning up the heat, and getting focused. Grab a fragrance or an essential oil infused with some of these spices when you're in need of a confidence boost or want to leave a lasting impression on a special someone:

- Black Pepper
- Cardamom
- Coriander
- Ginger
- Star Anise

Musky

Heady, sensual, and hard to resist, musky scents tend to activate the part of the brain connected to sex drive and intimacy. Grab a fragrance or an essential oil that features some of these notes when you're in the mood to seduce a crush—or seduce the masses:

- Amber
- Ambrette Seed
- Cedar
- Leather
- Musk

Herbal

As the zodiac sign whose birthday month coincides with the spring equinox, herb-based fragrances evoke your fresh and youthful approach to life and love. Go for fragrances or essential oils that feature these herbal notes when you're ready to reenergize your love life and start anew or when you need to clear stagnant vibes:

- Basil
- Fern
- Rosemary
- Tobacco
- Valerian

DAILY AFFIRMATIONS FOR LOVE

With your new signature scents at the ready, you are almost equipped to step out that door toward true love. Before you do, though, you should consider adding another tool to your tool belt. Daily affirmations are a great resource in helping you stay the course toward your dreams. These motivational phrases not only ensure that you are putting out the positive vibes that will draw opportunities to you but also remind you of just how deserving you are of a healthy, fulfilling relationship.

In astrology, there's an affirmation for Aries: "I am." With courage and unbridled power, Aries represents the life force that exists within us all and the unabashed expression of that life force. When you speak the words "I am," you are invoking that life force, while also stating something in that moment to be your truth. That's why the following affirmations incorporate "I am"—because an important component of love and attraction focuses on the affirmation of self. There's a reason why confidence is so sexy.

- I am loved and worthy of love as I am.
- I am sexy, vivacious, and inspiring; people can't get enough of me.
- I am in control of my love life and connect easily with those who are meant for me.
- I am patient with myself and know that I am not in a competition with anyone when it comes to getting the love I want.

- I am capable of having a happy, healthy, and loving relationship.
- I am able to make room for another person in my life without losing my independence.

DEALING WITH HEARTBREAK AND BREAKUPS

You've got your power colors and scents and your confidence-boosting affirmations—but what if love just doesn't go the way you want? Heartbreak happens, but fear not: you can bounce back and rekindle your fire after these bumps in the road.

Let's face it; having your heart broken is par for the course in this crazy thing called life. Fortunately, when you look at relationships through the lens of astrology you can see where the trouble might happen between partners before the trouble actually happens. With the help of astrology, you can give more forethought to how you engage and connect with others. While a heartbreak isn't always avoidable, there are times when you can avoid having your heart stepped on by being more thoughtful and intentional about those you choose to give your heart to.

For a fearless and free-spirted Aries like you, this may mean being more discerning about rushing headfirst into a relationship without knowing what you're getting into. Not that you should start doubting yourself or the decisions you make, but, as a go-getter Aries, you may need to take more time before making a choice in love. Part of this includes learning to read subtle verbal and nonverbal cues and feedback, as well as understanding the actions and intentions of a potential partner to make sure you're both on the same page. Weighing the pros and cons of a potential relationship can also be helpful in determining if someone is the right match for you.

If you are faced with a breakup, however, your Aries impulsiveness and need to stay on the move can be very helpful, as keeping yourself busy will help you to move on faster. While you don't like to deal with breakups any more than the other zodiac signs do, you have the capacity to bounce back from one quicker than the average person. One reason for this is that as a fire sign, you don't have the time or energy to waste crying over spilled milk, so you won't allow yourself to sit still for long enough to do so. Plus, if someone is crazy enough to let you go, Aries, they probably couldn't keep up anyway. Still, there's something to be said for taking responsibility for your actions when it comes to your relationships. For you, Aries, this may be learning to admit when you're wrong or recognizing that there's another person in the room with you who has their own needs, feelings, and desires for you to consider.

HANDLING RELATIONSHIPS WITH FAMILY AND FRIENDS

The meaning of family is one that you don't take lightly. You more than likely grew up in a tight-knit brood, where family traditions and history are something you're proud of and happily carry on with a sense of duty. As an assertive and intrepid sign, you're naturally inclined to protect those who you love. While Aries can get pegged as being selfish, you're willing to go above and beyond for those you call kin, donning your superhero cape for a family member in need.

Watch out for becoming too emotionally invested in the needs or demands of others, however, especially when it comes at the risk of ignoring your own emotional needs. This can create an imbalance that leaves you feeling taken for granted and less able to be vulnerable with others. Addressing this requires you to set boundaries for yourself and to admit when you're hurt or in need of some emotional support. Setting boundaries may mean letting people come to you and ask you for help first instead of swooping in to save the day. That way you don't end up feeling like you always have to be the one to rescue others. Giving people space to ask you for help means that you're also giving them agency to handle their own problems without butting in where you may not be needed or appreciated for your help.

Plus, if you're always the one to come to the rescue, when do people get to come to your rescue? As an independent Aries, asking for support may not be the easiest thing for you to do, but the more you practice with it, the easier it gets. Start with something small like asking a friend to help you with something around the house or to take a look at a resume you're sending out. Work your way up to the bigger tasks. Remember that people genuinely want to help others, and it feels good for them to do so.

When it comes to your friendships, you're often the spark plug of the group, entertaining your friends with your wild antics, feats of bravery, and raucous sense of humor. Being a natural go-getter, you often inspire and encourage your friends to be the best that they can be, especially during those times when they may not be feeling their best. Still, sometimes you have to remember the art of listening, as you can quickly become bored when your friends relay their problems and will often try to push them into doing what you think they should do. Remember that not everyone handles their problems the way that you do, Aries. Sometimes a person just needs to be heard. Some of your best friends are loyal, nurturing, and come in clutch during your time of need. They also teach you the importance of sharing, compromising, and keeping your ego from getting the best of you, as these are the friends that will let you know (with love) when you're being too bossy and will still be there for you despite your best efforts to show-case how strong and invulnerable you are.

That being said, you're not the type that needs to keep in contact with your friends on a daily basis, and, therefore, you need people in your life that don't take your need for independence personally. You also need friends that can hold their own when it comes to keeping up with you and your active schedule: when you're not out and about having fun, you're busy channeling all that energy and ambition into your work. This is what makes you such a boss!

YOUR APPROACH TO CAREER

As one of the biggest go-getters of the zodiac, you pursue your ambitions and career goals with a dogged determination and focus, refusing to take no for an answer. This is why you may find yourself at the helm of a company or in a managerial position, leading and inspiring your team toward success. Even if you're not in a position of leadership, there still needs to be an element of autonomy to what you do, as you're the kind of person who needs to be in charge. Careers that offer you a bit of danger and adventure (think professional race car driver Danica Patrick) are also appealing to you, as every Aries has a bit of a daredevil within. No matter what kind of work you choose to pursue, your career has to be something that stokes your fire and provides you with a mission in which you can take charge.

When it comes to pursuing the career that you desire, remember to keep your eye on the target and go for what you want, guns blazing. Still, as the firecracker you are, you can lose momentum when your plans don't take off as fast as you want them to. But not to worry, with a few affirmations you'll be back on track and manifesting the opportunities you want in no time!

DAILY AFFIRMATIONS TO HELP YOU GET AHEAD

Job searching can be tough, even for a confident self-starter like you. Waiting on people to respond to your application can be a drain on your enthusiasm and motivation as is receiving a rejection. As an Aries, you want what you want—like, *yesterday*. But the reality of job searching means that it can take time. This is also true when it comes to your goals and plans in your everyday work life. Using the power of affirmation is helpful when it comes to staying positive. You might even find that you get what you want faster. The following are affirmations chosen specifically for you as an Aries.

- Whatever I set out to do, I can accomplish.
- I am an innovator, a leader, and a force to be reckoned with in my field.
- I am passionate about my work and bring my A game to all I do.
- I am in charge of my professional life; I choose healthy work environments that fuel and empower me.
- I know that my success doesn't depend on winning or losing but on my ability to give my best.
- I have healthy outlets, like exercise to channel my frustration.
- People want to work with me because they know I am more than capable of getting the job done.

JOURNAL PROMPTS

While there will always be unavoidable obstacles or challenges to face on your road to success, it's important to remember that you have resources at your disposal to overcome these roadblocks. Affirmations are one great resource, but ultimately *you* are the main resource. With the following journal prompts you'll explore how you can use your personal and professional experiences to achieve success.

When faced with an obstacle, your first inclination as a headstrong Aries is to rush in and take action. However, if you don't approach the situation from a more thoughtful and intentional place, you can end up getting easily frustrated or stuck. Due to this impatience, you can be exceptionally hard on yourself when your plans don't pan out as quickly as you like. The following prompts will help you in examining where you currently are in your career and how you can approach challenges with the kind of forethought and patience you need.

- What kind of legacy do you want to leave? In what ways are you working toward building this legacy? In what ways can you start?
- When it comes to teamwork, what do you think is your greatest strength? Where would you like to improve?
- Have you ever turned a mistake into an opportunity? How might you be able to reframe a current challenge or a misstep into a silver lining? For example, a missed opportunity might open the door for you to take advantage of one elsewhere or give you the chance to build up your skills so you are actually ready for the kind of opportunity you're looking for.

DEALING WITH DISAPPOINTMENT

Still, disappointments are not always avoidable, and it is hard to not lose heart when things don't work out. Luckily, there are ways to deal with these setbacks without losing your drive. If there's one thing that you hate, it's losing. Being born with a competitive spirit and a need to win can be both a gift and a curse for you, especially since there are times when no matter how hard you try, you will still come up short. Part of dealing with disappointment means reframing your concept of winning and losing. Oftentimes, the idea of winning is rooted in external rewards that say very little about the real you, while losing means the lack of these rewards based on personal failure or laziness. That's not to say that you shouldn't want nice things, but unless you're willing to shift your value system to focus on what's really important, like striving to bring your best self to all that you do, then you'll always depend on outside validation.

While a healthy sense of competition can keep you motivated to push yourself and overcome your challenges, someone else's win doesn't make you a failure. So how can you avoid seeing yourself as such? One way to deal with this disappointment is by being aware of your need for instant gratification. While getting what you want without issue can feel great, instant gratification can be a side effect of a fear of missing out. Sometimes when you don't get the things that you want right away, it's important to recognize that there's a good reason for this—a reason that you might not immediately see. Perhaps "missing out" on an opportunity and finding something better—maybe you would have been hired for the job, only to find out that it was not what you signed up for, or that it wasn't the right fit for you. By reducing your need to fight for every single thing that comes your way, you create space for the better things that are meant for you. Taking this kind of approach means that you understand that there is more than enough good stuff to go around. This is especially important to remember during those times when you may be feeling stuck, desperate, or at a loss.

YOUR APPROACH TO WELLNESS

As an on-the-go fire sign, you thrive on excitement, adventure, and lots and lots of physical activity. This means that when it comes to self-care, it's important that you do activities that stoke your fabulous flames and keep you energized, entertained, and upbeat, like a game of softball (or virtually any competitive sport that you enjoy) with friends. And since your sign is linked with a warrior deity, you thrive on activities that push you to your physical limits and motivate you to stay disciplined, like training for an obstacle race or a marathon. If exercise and fitness are not necessarily your jam, you still need to engage the outlets that let your inner child out to play, such as old-school activities like bowling and go-karting. But before you set off on your next adventure, it's important to have spaces within your home where you can reenergize.

MAKING YOUR HOME YOUR CASTLE

Because of the amount of energy that you expend on a daily basis, it's important that you have a quiet and cozy home base that allows you to recharge your batteries. When decorating, add some of these elements to your home to give you the calm and reenergizing you need:

- Fresh flowers or plants that evoke a spring-like atmosphere. As a spring baby, it helps to surround yourself with items that evoke the beauty of the season, like bright red poppies or a succulent green aloe plant.
- Greens, browns, and other earth tones in the bedroom for a more restful sleep. Colors that are symbolic of earth can help you feel calm and grounded.
- Warm lighting, especially in places like the living room or bedroom, to help you calm down and relax. Warm light tends to have a sandman effect on the body.
- Artwork that features tranquil outdoor settings.
- Oranges, yellows, and other warm colors in places where you tend to be busiest, like a home office or kitchen.
- A kitchen filled with snacks and nutritious foods, like fresh fruits, chia-seed smoothies, and all-natural energy bars to help you refuel.

- A cozy nook or your special place on the couch for when you need to cocoon yourself away (if you share a home with others).

REKINDLING THE FIRE: TIPS FOR RECLAIMING YOUR SPARK

Of course, sometimes you may still feel zapped of your fire, and that's okay—you can put the pep back into your step in no time with a few energizing activities. You might approach the world like a superhero, but it doesn't mean you're superhuman. There are times when you hit a wall and need a pick-me-up or confidence boost. The following are tips on what to do when you're feeling like you've lost your spark.

Get Your Blood Pumping

With revved-up Mars as your ruling planet (the planet associated with fast cars and quick tempers), it's important that you incorporate regular physical activity into your schedule (if not daily, then as frequently as you possibly can) to avoid having to deal with the repercussions of restless or pent-up energy (e.g., temper tantrums). Bonus points if the activity requires you to punch, kick, or hit something, as every Aries needs to feed the warrior within. A good sweat can be just the thing you need to clear your mind and feel rejuvenated.

Do Something That Scares You a Little

That adrenaline rush that comes with doing something outside of your comfort zone is just the thing you need to boost your confidence and leave you feeling like yourself again. This could be something like taking skydiving lessons or exploring a new city or part of the country alone. This could also mean doing something a bit more intimate like sharing something that you've never told anyone with a friend or telling a very personal story via a blog post or essay.

Have Sex

This might be self-explanatory, but as the sign under the planet that rules passion, a good romp in the sack could be just the thing you need to get your creative juices flowing while boosting your confidence and endorphins. Medical studies have shown that sex also alleviates stress and lowers your blood pressure, which helps to keep any hotheaded Aries cool. P.S. Self-pleasure counts.

Watch an Action-Packed Movie

When you're having a hard time getting your engines running, sometimes all you need to do is watch a movie (or two) to help inspire you back into action. Even better if the movie stars a butt-kicking demigoddess like Wonder Woman or a sword-wielding maven like Beatrix Kiddo of *Kill Bill*.

Eat Something Spicy

Spicy foods that incorporate ingredients like peppers, chili powder, or curry help to wake up the senses and stimulate the nervous system. When you eat spicy foods (as hot as you can stand) it's like giving your body a boost, helping to stoke the fire within.

KEEPING COOL UNDER FIRE: TIPS FOR RELIEVING STRESS

Now that the fire is burning, watch out for flames getting a bit too high! Fortunately, when a burnout is on the way there are a few simple ways to tame the fire. Physically, your zodiac sign is associated with the head and the muscles, parts of the body where actions are initiated and carried out; astrologically, your sign is symbolized by the ram and the element of fire. This means you have to be mindful of not rushing headfirst into things and letting your fire burn out of control. This impulsive part of your nature can manifest as tension headaches, irritability, or fatigue caused by the inability to slow down and get proper rest. At the same time, it can also make you accident prone—knocking things over, colliding with people on the street, or even getting into a minor car accident (or a close call).

The antidote is adding a little Venus and Mercury into your life for balance. In astrology Venus represents the opposite of Mars. Where Mars represents anger, passion, fast-moving things like cars, and masculine energy, Venus represents peace and harmony, beauty like flowers and jewels, sensual pleasure, and feminine energy. Associated with discernment and discipline, Mercury is the planet people turn to when they need to think things through. Try to incorporate these Venus- and Mercury-related activities as a regular part of your schedule.

Watch What You Eat

If you're constantly in a rush to get where you're going, it can be a challenge to make sure that you're eating right and eating enough. It doesn't take any crazy dieting; it's simply about being more in tune with your body. For example, try paying closer attention to how you feel when you consume certain foods and drinks, like those that are high in processed sugar or caffeine. How does your body respond? What happens to your mood?

Be Picky

As a self-starter with tons of energy to burn, you rarely have a hard time finding new projects to begin or activities to get yourself involved in. While your go-getter attitude and self-initiative are key pieces of your impressive arsenal of strengths, you don't need to take everything and anything on simply because you've got the energy to do so. It's okay to be picky about how you spend your time: this is how you avoid spreading yourself too thin and burning out.

Open Your Eyes

What catches your eye? What do you enjoy looking at? Is it a pretty painting? A green garden? The open sky? While the act of slowing down can be hard to do in a world that's constantly moving forward, it is helpful to practice the art of being in the moment. You are allowing your mind to rest and your body to relax. One way to do this is by focusing your gaze on something you find aesthetically pleasing. Then, push your gaze a step deeper by taking in the colors you see. Are there different hues? What about the texture? Is it shiny and smooth, or matte and rough? What stands out to you the most about what you see and why? Also make note of how you feel. Do you feel more relaxed? Amused? Excited?

Slow Down

You're probably rolling your eyes at this, and you're well within your right to do so as the speedster of the zodiac. Nevertheless, do you ever notice that sometimes when you bring a rushed or harried kind of energy into something you're doing, it ends up making the activity worse, and you are left feeling frustrated? Yeah, that's the signal that you need to slow down. Sometimes something as simple as taking a breath and counting to three can make a big difference between getting a task done and getting a task done right. On another note, if you're always in a rush, you may fail to tune in to the intuitive signals or feelings that can help you make clearheaded decisions. For example, there may be a reason why you were initially hesitant about saying yes to attending an event you heard about or taking on an opportunity your boss offered to you. That hesitant feeling is your intuition telling you to avoid taking on something that you'll regret later.

Honor Your Feelings

Feeling happy? Okay. Feeling angry, sad, or afraid? That's okay too. Don't try to stifle your feelings or rush yourself to get over them too quickly. Give yourself permission to experience the full range of your emotions. It's often better to let a feeling pass than to try to ignore it, as it only prolongs the feeling. While emotions are associated more with the power of the Moon than Venus, they also help to connect you to your intuition, find clarity in a situation, live authentically, and show you where you may need to take better care of yourself.

CHAPTER 2
TAURUS: APRIL 20–MAY 20

A lusty yet down-to-earth sign, you know how to get the most out of life (whether it's a five-star meal, extra zeros on a paycheck, or relationships that stand the test of time) by staying cool under pressure and barely breaking a sweat. You have the kind of sticking power that others envy, making you the ideal example of what patience and perseverance can accomplish. That's why, when it comes to maintaining your sense of security and well-being, you need supports at the ready that can help to keep you calm and grounded in the face of uncertainty and this constantly changing world.

   In this chapter, you will find examples of those supports, along with tips for ramping up your magnetism so you can further attract the things that you want in life, from a healthy, romantic relationship to your dream career.

(YOU'RE) A BRICK HOUSE

Sensual. Grounded. Determined. These are just some of the words used to describe the earthy, palpable mojo that you were born with. The throwback song "Brick House" by the Commodores is also appropriate. Famous Taureans like Janet Jackson, Queen Elizabeth II, and Stevie Wonder are but a few examples of the influence and resolve that those born under the sign of Taurus wield.

As a zodiac sign associated with the element of earth, much of your focus is rooted here in the material world, where you strive to achieve and maintain stability and financial security. You're largely concerned with building things that last, from relationships to career. Blessed with creativity and a Midas touch, you show the rest of us how to create and live the good life—turning everything you set your mind to into gold through hard work and your keen understanding of the five senses. You need to be sure that what you're investing in is worth your time and energy; you'll barely lift a finger if you know something or someone isn't worth it. Though once you are invested, you're loyal to a fault (more on that later). Being ruled by Venus, the mythological goddess of love, beauty, and pleasure, the physical body is also your playground—whether alone or with a partner. While you can go between dressing up and dressing down (depending on your level of comfort), you never miss the chance to adorn yourself with high-end baubles and fabrics.

Despite all your beauty and perseverance, some of your biggest challenges center on an inability to let go and adapt to change. This can lead to staying in situations well past their prime, out of a fear of uncertainty or complacency. While you can be a trailblazer, unafraid to rock the boat when it comes to pursuing something you believe in or maintaining your principles, you can also risk losing some of that moxie if you feel like you might lose your security. This isn't to suggest that you shouldn't want to live comfortably or move at your own pace, but a lack of movement can lead to a stagnation that denies you the opportunity for personal growth.

Meanwhile, by living in a world that often pushes you to place your self-worth on external rewards, it's hard as a materially driven zodiac sign to not do the same. As a result, your self-esteem could take a blow if, for example, you feel like you're not making the right amount of money or can't buy the luxury items you crave. In response, you may believe that you should accept less than what you deserve, or you may take on a by-any-means-necessary approach that can turn you into a workaholic or make you fearful of leaving a bad situation like a toxic job if it means temporarily taking a pay cut. But fear not, in this chapter, you'll discover how to better live by your own value system and respond to the changes that life tosses your way.

YOUR APPROACH TO LOVE

There's a reason why Taureans are so irresistible: you're sensual, down-to-earth partners who take pride in providing pleasure, comfort, and stability for a partner. You're looking for these very same qualities in your significant other, too, as you long for love that can last and last and last. Not the type to jump headfirst into a relationship, you prefer to take your time and have a love interest prove themselves worthy. This makes you a pragmatist when it comes to your heart, though you are still quite the romantic. As a child of Venus, you need someone that can wine and dine you and satisfy your top-dollar taste. It's not that you're demanding—you just know what you like, and if an admirer is paying attention, they'll know what you like too.

WOWING WITH COLOR

Of course, being a child of Venus means that you're no stranger to romance and seduction, but even a supreme partner like you should have a few extra delights up your sleeve to attract the kind of significant other you want.

Engaging the five senses is something that you know how to do—and you do it well. But did you know that your sign also has its own signature colors that boost your magnetism? Look to these colors to amplify your luxe charm.

Coral

Incorporating both red and orange, coral is associated with warmth and feel-good vibes, traits that are also associated with your zodiac sign. Add this color to your wardrobe when you want to brighten or complement your natural glow. Admirers and potential dates will hardly be able to resist you.

Cream

Timeless, decadent, chic—these are just a few of the words to describe this neutral shade. Similar to white, cream is also associated with peace and purity. While some may consider it boring, as a Taurus you have the style sense to pull it off. Wear it when you want to look like a million bucks, without the lofty price tag.

Green

Associated with wealth and fertility, green is a power color for you. Why? Because it represents everything that Taurus stands for. Put shades of green in rotation in your wardrobe when you're looking to draw in or align with the energy of wealth and abundance.

SCENTS FOR POWER AND SEDUCTION

As you know well, there's more than one sense to engage when it comes to seduction. Being a connoisseur of luxury and pleasure, you need signature scents that not only appeal to your senses, but also represent opulence, decadence, and eroticism, evoking romance in your life.

Woody

Fragrances with woody notes are warm, sensual, and appeal to those with an earthy kind of energy—just like you. Use fragrances or essential oils that contain these notes when you're in a seductive mood:

- Moss
- Oakmoss
- Patchouli
- Sandalwood
- Vetiver

Floral

As a spring baby, you need scents that represent your lush beauty and romantic spirit. Florals satiate the senses and evoke an idyllic atmosphere, like a wide-open meadow or a rich, vibrant garden. Wear these notes when you're ready to make magic happen:

- Daisy
- Freesia
- Lily
- Orchid
- Rose

Sweet

Also known as *gourmand* scents, these make for fragrances that are as delicious as they are sexy—a perfect fit for your taste for decadence. Call on these notes when you're ready to leave your admirers hungry for more:

- Caramel
- Chocolate
- Fig
- Honey
- Sugar

DAILY AFFIRMATIONS FOR LOVE

After catching eyes and tantalizing admirers with your sweet scents, it's time to align your body with your mind to attract the healthy, fulfilling relationships you deserve. Daily affirmations help you to attract the love life that you want by ensuring that you put out positive vibes. Affirmations also serve as a reminder of what you are and are not looking for in a partner, so even when love is blind, *you* are not.

As the zodiac sign represented by the bull, it's safe to say that you often don't do anything until you're good and ready. However, when you are ready, you throw all your energy into whatever you choose to do. Your love life is no different: you prefer to take your time before rushing into anything. Sometimes, though, it is easy to settle for a mismatched partner out of fear of not having the stability and security you crave. The love affirmations that follow encourage you to be intentional with your love mojo and who you attract with it. As someone of exquisite taste, you can improve your odds of attracting partners who are worth your time and energy by using these love affirmations to send a clear message out into the world about what you value. At the same time, these affirmations will help you hold yourself accountable to your standards:

- I am worthy of a stable, committed relationship filled with romance and joy.
- I am worthy of a devoted and loving partner.
- I am worthy of a sensual and physically pleasurable relationship.
- I am worthy of a partner who is generous with affection and is financially stable.
- I am worthy of a partner who encourages me to step out of my comfort zone.

DEALING WITH HEARTBREAK AND BREAKUPS

As prepared as you may be, heartbreak is a part of love that most cannot avoid. Fortunately, there are ways to deal with heartbreak head-on (just like a bull). As one of the most loyal and steadfast signs of the zodiac, you commit your heart to someone and there's very little that can change that. This means that even if a relationship is over, it's still never really over for you, as you don't let go of a relationship or an ex easily. Once you've taken someone as yours, they are yours forever. Holding on to a relationship out of a fear of upsetting what you've built does little to serve your happiness. The same thing can be said for holding on to a grudge against an ex: all the energy that you're giving to resenting that person is blocking you from opening yourself up to someone who is better suited for you. Though dealing with a breakup or a heartbreak is never pleasant, the strength and determination that you were born with will help you to move on from a bad relationship rather than try to force it to work or your partner to change.

It's important to remember that if a relationship does end, it doesn't mean that you've put in the work for nothing or that you've failed. To be able to connect with another person in a mature, loving relationship means work—working on ourselves and the relationship. Your willingness to stick with what you start is a gift, but that gift should be used judiciously. Sometimes there are romantic relationships that are only meant to last for a short period of time. These short-lived romances don't always have to cause heartbreak and damage: they can be used as valuable experiences to teach us something about ourselves as partners, our relationship needs, and what we value in a significant other. If you do find yourself having a hard time letting go of someone, remind yourself that you can have what you shared with this person again.

HANDLING RELATIONSHIPS WITH FAMILY AND FRIENDS

As someone who cares for the well-being of others, you are a comforting, supportive presence in the lives of those you love. There's a reason why you're considered the "rock" to friends and family; you are willing to offer a hearty meal, a comfortable couch, or a few extra dollars to anyone in need. While there's a part of you that thrives on being needed, being taken for granted is something that you need to be mindful of, as it can make you vulnerable to people who only want to take from you and never give back. This isn't to say that you shouldn't be generous, but you should recognize that you don't always have to be the nice guy (or gal).

As a child of Venus, the planet associated with charm and the art of getting along with others, you loathe being seen as the "bad guy" when it comes to your relationships. You might even find yourself going out of your way so as not to come off as mean or selfish. However, it's important to understand that relating to others isn't always going to be pretty. Sometimes you have to be the "bad guy" and accept your position as such. Self-worth means respecting yourself by putting your needs and desires before others when need be. This is how you avoid resentment, as toxic feelings build up when you overextend yourself. That's why it's okay for you to say no and to save a little something for yourself by setting clear boundaries. Those who truly love you, whether they're friends or family, will acknowledge and accept your boundaries because they won't value you solely by how much you do for them.

YOUR APPROACH TO CAREER

Your loyalty, generosity, and strength are true gifts when it comes to the people you love, and it may surprise you to learn that those same gifts will benefit you in other parts of your life, such as the workplace.

As the sign associated with financial abundance, you aren't truly happy in your career unless it offers you two things: 1. long-term security, and 2. the chance to make a difference in the lives of others. This is why you are often drawn to positions like financial adviser, agricultural engineer, luxury fashion designer, or sommelier. These careers offer tenure, an attractive retirement package, or the opportunity to inspire change and leave your own indelible mark on the world. Since Venus, your planetary ruler, is also in charge of arts and culture, you may also be a musician, singer, fine artist, or chef.

Your hard work, persistence, and skill help you turn whatever you do into gold. Because of how much of yourself you're willing to put into your work, you need a career where you feel like a valued member of the team, from your daily work environment to your paycheck. You not only want to be seen as a thought leader, creator, or trendsetter in your field, you want to know that the work you're doing is making an impact on the lives of others. If you're working for a company that makes you feel like just another cog in the wheel, you're going to be unhappy. When you feel that you are valued for your work and the work you do has meaning, you are willing to give 110 percent.

DAILY AFFIRMATIONS TO HELP YOU GET AHEAD

Daily affirmations are a great tool in helping you stay on the path toward the career positions and achievements you truly want. These motivational phrases not only ensure that you are putting out the positive vibes that will draw opportunities to you, but also remind you of things to recall when taking on a new job, working toward a promotion, or reconsidering your current position.

As a Taurus, you have an almost uncanny ability to manifest money and financial opportunities thanks to your practical thinking, persistence, and personal magnetism. Though when you're stuck in an unhappy job situation, it can be easy for you to forget your power. Use the following affirmations as a daily reminder of how awesome you are and what you deserve in your professional life. When you believe something to be true (like your ability to manifest what you want), that belief will be reflected back to you through your experiences with the world around you.

- I am a true original. I am unafraid to go off the beaten path when it comes to my work and break new ground.
- I am worthy of having a career that I love and that pays me well.
- I have valuable skills and ideas to offer; others would kill for a chance to work with me.
- I bring ideas to the table that are original and inventive. I am respected for my intelligence and my trendsetting methods.
- With my dedication and perseverance, I can do anything I put energy into.
- I honor my creative energy and my need for autonomy. I choose opportunities that are the right match for me.
- I have a Midas touch: whatever I do I can it turn into gold.
- My work makes a true difference in the lives of others.

JOURNAL PROMPTS

In addition to these affirmations, it will also help you in pursuing your career goals to draw on the experiences that have brought you to where you are now. Use the following prompts to explore these past situations and discover what it is that you are looking for now.

Being a Taurus means that you desire stability. Job-hopping or having long stretches of time between jobs is something that makes you feel antsy and unsettled. However, your need for stability can sometimes keep you locked in positions where you feel creatively stuck, uninspired, or undervalued. Here are a few guiding questions to help you examine where you may be stuck and how to move forward:

- Where might you need to take a risk in your career?
- What do you do when things feel stagnant? How can you tell when it's time to shake things up?
- What kind of impact would you like to make on the world around you? What's one step you can take now to align with this vision?

DEALING WITH DISAPPOINTMENT

You've recited the affirmations and read through the prompts—but the vision you have for your career still isn't coming into fruition like you hoped it would. It is hard not to lose your motivation. However, before you exchange that shot at an executive office for a spot on your couch, let's talk about how to deal with career setbacks.

One special thing about being a Taurus is that if a way to getting what you want isn't readily provided to you, you have no problems with making your own way. This is something for you to remember should you ever find yourself feeling bad about your current job situation. You have the power to write your own narrative when it comes to your happiness and success. The same way you shouldn't hold on to disappointment when it comes to a romantic relationship, you shouldn't hold on to disappointment in your professional life either. After all, Venus, your planetary ruler, is in charge of both relationships and money. When you recognize how much you're truly worth, you are better at attracting opportunities that are right for you instead of lamenting and being angry over the ones that aren't.

Remember, Taurus: don't let fear or uncertainty keep you from living a truly fulfilled life.

Sticking with a job that offers little value or meaning out of fear that it would be too difficult to find something better is a trap that you can learn to avoid. Try reframing or challenging the lack you see in your life by affirming the abundance or resources that you do have. For example, can you make a list of at least five things you're grateful for today? If you have something to be grateful for then it's a good chance that you have resources available to you.

Another way that you can affirm the abundance in your life is by affirming yourself. Recognize that you deserve the kind of fulfillment that extends far beyond material wealth. Try this as an exercise: come up with at least five things that you enjoy that are unrelated to money or material wealth. Overall, any professional relationship that you choose to pursue should be reciprocal. In other words, you should get more out of a job than just a paycheck. Yes, money is important but so is being happy with what you do on a daily basis, even during moments on the job that may be challenging. This balance will also be important when looking at your personal well-being, and the divide you must establish between work and home life.

YOUR APPROACH TO WELLNESS

As a Taurus, you are usually on one of two sides of the spectrum: either you kick back and take it easy or you enjoy a busy, active lifestyle; there is no in-between. Regardless of which wellness style you fall under, your *ultimate* goal is to feel good. Inside every Taurus lives a lounge lizard that loves getting cozy on his or her favorite chair or spot on the couch, so it's crucial to keep that chillaxed vibe going in your home.

MAKING YOUR HOME YOUR CASTLE

Since you need a home base that provides you with a place to luxuriate, create, and entertain—playing as hard as you work—here are a few guidelines for crafting your dream space. Use these items to keep the energy in your home bright and happy:

- Warm colors like oranges and yellows; lush jewel tones like emerald green, ruby red, and citrine yellow. These vitalizing colors can help to stimulate creativity, lift a bad mood, promote the flow of financial abundance, and break up stale energy in your living space.
- Plush fabrics and textures like velvet, sequins, and faux fur are also good for a tactile and sensual sign like you. These fabrics are not only pleasing to the eye but also pleasing to the touch.
- Decorative items with gold accents and trimming, as gold represents opulence.
- Vivid, eye-catching artwork that can be a source of beauty, inspiration, and calming vibes.
- Lots of green plants and bright flowers, which represent fresh, opulent, and fertile energy.
- Mirrors to open up the space—and give you a reason to check yourself out.
- A designated space where you can create, whether it's through cooking, painting, etc. Having your own space for your creative projects will allow you to clear your head and relax with something you enjoy doing.

STAYING GROUNDED: TIPS TO KEEP YOUR FOOTING

As an earth sign, the material world is where you house your identity. That includes your relationship to your physical body. Therefore, during times when you feel off-kilter and you're in need of comfort, you tend to prefer activities that bring you back into your body, whether it's through touch, taste, sight, scent, or sound. Being aware of your body and the sensations that you feel within it will help to ground you back down in the physical plane. Still, sometimes you may feel a bit overwhelmed by the world. Fortunately, there are simple ways to stay grounded when you "just can't even."

As a stability-loving zodiac sign, you're apt to dig your feet in and refuse to budge when faced with making a drastic or necessary change. So, when the chaos of the world swirling around you throws you off-balance, your energy and self-confidence are drained. Don't fret—the following are easy ways to get your footing back.

Get Body Work
Whether it's receiving a full body massage, acupuncture, or a hair-shampooing by a significant other, the power of touch is a great way to relieve and release tension in the body. As a Taurus—and as an earth sign—it is easy for you to hold on to things, whether physical or emotional, so you need to pay extra attention to how you carry stress in your body.

Eat Something Indulgent
While moderation is key, eating a decadent treat like chocolate ice cream or a rich meal like cheesy lasagna can be just the pleasurable escape you need—and a tasty reward for a hard day's work. It's not just about the taste alone: taking a moment to be present in a meal helps you to slow down and find your bearings.

Make Something with Your Hands
The process and feel of creating something by hand can have a calming, soothing effect while calling on just about all your senses. At the same time, it also gets your creative juices flowing, which is key for a Venus-ruled sign

like you. Creative energy connects you to your sense of vitality, passion, and enthusiasm, thereby helping you to feel like yourself again.

Try Sensation Play

Feathers, blindfolds, ice, spankings—these are just a few examples of the sensations that can be given to or received from a partner to ramp up sexual pleasure in the bedroom. Not only is sensation play an activity that engages all five senses, helping you stay grounded in the present moment, but it can also help you to experience your body in new, pleasurable ways.

Return to Nature

As an earth sign, especially one born during the spring, connecting with the actual earth is rejuvenating for you. Walk barefoot in the grass, do a few body rolls in an open field, or have a picnic in a garden or under a lush tree. If the season or weather calls for something indoors, try a public greenhouse or atrium.

TENDING THE EARTH: TIPS FOR RELIEVING STRESS

Getting back into your earthly element helps with relieving day-to-day strains as well. And let's face it—life can be stressful! Luckily, there are a few other ways to further ease these anxieties. Being an earth sign means that you like to keep the things in your life familiar and in their place. As a Taurus, you don't fancy abrupt changes or being met with uncertainty. This is why stress shows up for you when you're thrown into situations that require some form of change or adaptability. As a response to the stress, you might find yourself feeling stuck, lethargic, unable to let things go, or overindulging in the things that bring you comfort—like food. However, as you know, change is necessary to growth, and the more you resist it, the harder it is to manage and adapt to the shifts that take place in your life.

The tips that follow are designed to help you better handle change so you can get unstuck and start moving again.

Clear the Clutter

Often clutter is the result of fear of letting something go or of losing a sense of security. At the same time, clutter can also pile up during times when you are feeling stuck, overwhelmed, or uninspired. While you don't have to toss everything out in one fell swoop, try starting with the things that you no longer use and items that you can afford to donate. By releasing old things from your life, you are signaling to the universe you are ready to welcome in something much better for you, like a new opportunity or even a relationship.

Aromatherapy

You of all people know how powerful the sense of smell can be; it can transport you to a place or a specific time and give you a boost of good feelings. Using spicy or pungent essential oils like lemongrass, peppermint, cinnamon, citrus, eucalyptus, or rosemary help rev up your energy and wake you up, while giving you the clarity and confidence to tackle any future challenges head-on.

Balance It Out

When you're stressed it's easy to go for your usual comforts like eating rich foods, drinking alcohol, or getting cozy in your favorite chair. While it's okay to treat yourself, you have to be careful with going overboard, as overindulgence and a lack of physical movement can throw your body out of whack and affect your mood. Try to balance out your comforts by adding in some exercise and nutritious meals, both of which will help you to combat stress and fatigue. No need to overdo it on the exercise either: just get into the habit of getting your body moving.

Adorn Yourself

When you're feeling stressed out or overwhelmed, you might be motivated to grab your favorite pair of sweats rather than your makeup bag. Don't take for granted how much the right shade of lipstick or pretty satin blouse can change your entire mood. Wearing things that are aesthetically pleasing and make you feel sexy is a great way for boosting feel-good hormones like serotonin. Taking the extra time to adorn or dress yourself in something nice is a simple way to take care of yourself.

CHAPTER 3
GEMINI: MAY 21–JUNE 20

As curious as you are multifaceted, you approach the world around you with a twinkle in your eye, a spring in your step, and a mind full of brilliant ideas. Not one to hold your tongue or wait around for those unable to keep up with your quick wit and on-the-go lifestyle, you pride yourself on knowing the right thing to say at the right time. You also have a knack for turning abstract concepts into concrete results. Once you put your mind to something, there's very little that can get in your way.

In this chapter, you will learn more about how you navigate through love, career, and self-care. You will also discover how to recapture your creative mojo when you feel like you're running in circles, stuck in place, or spread too thin. Like the element of air that represents your sign, this chapter will help keep you feeling fresh—without losing any cool points.

YOU'RE A WHIZ KID

As the zodiac sign associated with intellect and the art of communication, you thrive on thoughts, words, and education—learning as much as you can, whenever you can. Always with a funny anecdote or an interesting tidbit of information at the ready, you can often be found holding court over a crowd of people, entertaining them for hours on end with your wit. Associated with the element of air, you tend to need space (and lots of it) to come and go as you please. Even if you choose to settle down, you need a schedule (and an understanding partner) that enables you to stay on the move, picking up new experiences and knowledge as you go.

Also like the element of air, you strive to be in more than one place at one time, enjoying the freedom of movement. This also means that you identify most with all things trendy, fresh, and cutting-edge, often quick to lose interest in anything more than five minutes old. While this makes you an incredibly innovative, razor-sharp thinker, you must also be able to guard against boredom, overstimulation, and distraction. In a world that moves at hyper-speed, you have no trouble keeping up. It's the slowing down that throws you off. This extends to feelings too: when your mind is always busy processing every thought and emotion that filters through it, it becomes hard to find the time or the space to thoroughly and honestly feel what you feel.

You have a knack for juggling multiple projects, interests, and social circles in a way that would make another person's head spin. Not only do you pick up and absorb information at lightning speed, but you also possess the ability to think on your feet and adjust yourself accordingly to just about any situation at hand.

Being a sign of duality means that you have a gift for finding the common thread between abstract, conflicting, or unrelated ideas. This gift enables you to keep room in your life, in your head, or in your conversations for many things (and many people) at once. The challenge here, though, is to avoid spreading yourself too thin with too many interests, activities, or casual acquaintances. Overall, the key to your well-being and happiness lies in your duality; while you are learning to honor and express the many pieces that make you who you are, you are also learning how not to lose yourself in the fragments—especially when it comes to love.

YOUR APPROACH TO LOVE

Whip-smart with a bubbly disposition, you approach love with a childlike curiosity: flirting, having fun, and making eye-opening discoveries along the way. While you prefer to keep your connections light and sweet, every now and then you come across someone worth a little more investigation. Above all else, you need a partner who can make room for all your various interests as well as the various sides of your personality. No matter what kind of relationship you do choose, you need someone who's going to keep you surprised and intellectually titillated.

WOWING WITH COLOR

Although you're a connoisseur of words and conversation, you can maintain a little mystery and capture the attention of a love interest without even saying a thing. Wear the following colors to showcase your bubbly personality and your brilliant Gemini mind.

Blue

Go for crisp, vivid hues of blue when you want to make a statement, project confidence, and show the world that you know what you're doing. A power color for you, blue is associated with wisdom and clarity of mind.

Violet

Brilliant and eye-catching, violet is associated with intuition and spiritual attunement. Make this your go-to color when you want to create an air of magic or when you're in the mood to feel lavish, as this is a color connected to wealth too.

Yellow

A sunny color to match your sunny personality, yellow helps you to make a positive, lasting impression on your admirers while boosting your spirits too. Because of its association with joy and vitality, yellow is the perfect color to wear on a playful first date.

SCENTS FOR POWER AND SEDUCTION

As an intellectual Gemini, you experience seduction in your head first. Even the act of flirting relies on your wit and sharp sense of humor. Using more tangible elements such as color and scent will enable you to enhance those traits and boost your allure. To maintain your light and carefree attitude, look to fragrances that promote a fresh, flirty, and buoyant vibe. Use aromatic, citrusy, or fruity scents to find or create your signature scent; when you're in your element, you're virtually unstoppable.

Aromatic

Fragrances with aromatic notes are emotionally uplifting, yet have soothing properties as well. Wear fragrances and essential oils with these aromatic notes when you want to keep your cool while effortlessly driving your admirers mad:

- Basil
- Lavender
- Mint
- Sage
- Vervain

Citrus

Citrus notes are wonderful for you, because they promote mental clarity. Wearing perfumes or essential oils with these citrus-based ingredients can boost your confidence and stimulate your creative energy. These notes are also found in unisex fragrances—perfect for your dual nature:

- Bergamot
- Lemon
- Lime
- Mandarin

Fruity

Sweet, refreshing, yet also tantalizing enough to pique an admirer's curiosity, fragrances that contain fruity notes are not only mood boosters but also a nod to your playful spirit and bubbly personality:

- Mango
- Pineapple
- Plum
- Raspberry

DAILY AFFIRMATIONS FOR LOVE

Now that you've explored the benefits of a more sensual approach to romance, let's get back to what you love the most: words. Words are a big part of your problem-solving superpower as a Gemini: how you use them often determines your ability to develop solutions, create opportunities, and get what you want. Why should it be any different when it comes to your love life? Hint: it's not. Words, in many ways, are a form of power: they help to initiate an action, set a mood, and shift energy. When it comes to attracting love, the way you think and speak about it matters. If you believe that you will never find love or speak about love negatively (e.g., "everyone cheats"), then that becomes your truth. If you choose words that affirm the relationship that you want, that becomes your truth instead. The following affirmations focus on keeping the positive vibes flowing, while also serving as a reminder of the fulfilling love life that you deserve.

- I am ready to do the work it takes to maintain a happy, healthy relationship.
- I recognize that the right relationship for me is one that thrives on open communication and conversation.
- I understand that the right match for me will love me for my humor, intelligence, and bubbly attitude.
- I welcome a relationship where each day is an opportunity to share with and learn something new about my partner.
- I am ready for a relationship that pushes me to explore my deeper feelings in a safe, supportive way.
- I am ready for a partner that respects my ideas, my opinions, and my independence.

DEALING WITH HEARTBREAK AND BREAKUPS

It makes a lot of sense that Mercury (the winged messenger god) rules over Gemini: just like Mercury, you are known for your incomparable speed. You hardly ever stay in one place, especially if there's a threat of boredom or weighty matters looming overhead. While your need to stay on the move isn't a bad thing, it can become a barrier to having a happy, healthy relationship if not balanced with the grounding forces of responsibility and commitment. In other words, genuine connections with people require that you go beyond the surface level (like a pretty face or a casual, intermittent connection) When you avoid digging deeper out of fear of commitment and hard work, you can find yourself having a string of relationships that offer little substance or emotional depth. Instead, you'll find yourself inadvertently attracting partners who smother or attempt to control you or partners who are undependable.

Despite these tendencies, as an air sign you thrive on having a sense of connectedness with others. This also includes romantic connections based on mutual understanding and acceptance. However, because of your fear of true intimacy, it is easy for you to fall into a Mr./Ms. Right Now approach (as opposed to waiting for a true Mr./Ms. Right) which will leave you feeling unsatisfied after a while.

Part of getting past this tendency is understanding that experiencing true intimacy (and thus vulnerability) with another person is not a weakness or a loss of your freedom. Still, if you do find yourself heartbroken, one of the best things you can do is change your scenery, either through travel, a relaxing vacation from your busy schedule, or the world of a great book or film. The freedom that these options will afford you feels akin to breathing in fresh air, giving you the space and clarity to focus on something that truly matters: moving on.

HANDLING RELATIONSHIPS WITH FAMILY AND FRIENDS

While you hate being tied down to any one thing, your family is where you give a lot of your energy, often going above and beyond for the people you love. Despite your ease with helping loved ones, you often struggle with asking for help yourself, out of a fear of being seen as incapable of handling things on your own. While your self-sufficiency is impressive, it's important for you to recognize that not every burden has to be carried squarely on your shoulders alone. Sometimes two minds are better than one when solving a problem.

This goes for your friendships too. You may spread yourself too thin at times, trying to be everything to everyone, but that energy may not always be reciprocated as much as you like because of your apprehension to appearing needy and not in control. Who knew that such a brilliantly funny, multifaceted maven such as you could be, well, human? News flash, you are. And revealing who you really are allows people to better relate to you because you're being genuine.

This also applies to telling people how you feel. Instead of keeping things locked up in your head, where you end up mentally burning yourself out from overanalyzing every little detail, having trusted friends who you can talk to without fear of judgment is as important for you as learning how to honor your feelings. Look for the kind of people who push you to be your authentic self and who happily accept you for it, while providing the space for you to feel what you feel rather than trying to rationalize your way through it. If you find yourself in relationships where your friend's love or acceptance of you feels conditional, it may be time for you to rethink the relationship.

YOUR APPROACH TO CAREER

As a hub of communication and innovation, it's no surprise that you are drawn to careers that span the communication and tech fields, such as journalism, advertising, start-ups, and software engineering. Because of your gift for words and creative thinking, you may also find yourself in a career involving music or comedy. In fact, the list of celebrity Geminis is full of hilarious and creatively talented personalities including Prince, Lauryn Hill, and Amy Schumer. The fields you gravitate toward tend to be just as diverse and multifaceted as you are, calling on the multiple skills and interests you've developed along the way. You might even find yourself holding down more than one job at a time in very different industries.

Overall, you need a job that keeps you on your toes and changes pace or focus regularly. If you can travel or work remotely, you'll enjoy the job a lot more than if you were glued to a desk all day.

DAILY AFFIRMATIONS TO HELP YOU GET AHEAD

Using affirmations is a great way to attract the exciting, engaging career or job advancements that you want. Affirmations are also a great way to open yourself up to opportunities, encouraging positivity even when your career goals aren't panning out as you had hoped.

Despite being a sign that lives within the intellectual realm, you also need to have a spiritual connection to what you do for a living. Otherwise, your creativity and your enthusiasm will feel stunted. In other words, you need to believe in what you do. The following affirmations are geared toward helping you manifest these kinds of employment opportunities as well as affirm what *you're* bringing to the table.

- I am a great asset to any team; I'm sharp, witty, and brimming with talent. I have the power to impact and influence minds.
- I am constantly evolving; whatever I don't know I am willing to go out and learn.
- The right job for me encourages me to think creatively and outside the box.
- My career provides me with a fun and engaging workplace; no two days feel the same.
- I work with people who I enjoy being around; they're friendly and professional, and they understand the value of teamwork.
- I have a career that affords me a healthy work-life balance.
- I have a job that I love and that pays me well for my skills.

- I take my craft seriously and dedicate the time to improving my skills. I bring authenticity and integrity to everything I do.

JOURNAL PROMPTS

Journal prompts are also a great way to explore and solidify what you need and don't need in a career—which is good news for the zodiac sign that loves to write! As the astrological sign of communication, you of all people know the value of writing your thoughts down as a way to think things through and make a decision. The following questions encourage you to think about the changes that you'd like to see in your career and how you can make those changes happen based on what you've learned from prior experiences. When you have an analytical mind like yours, it helps to have perspective so you don't get lost in a loop of overanalysis. These questions encourage you to consider the small moving parts without losing sight of your bigger objectives:

- What's your biggest dream for your career? What are some steps you can take now to get closer to making it come true?
- What are some of the lessons you've learned that have helped you along your career path? In what ways are you actively applying those lessons to your everyday work life?
- When has taking a leap of faith worked for you? How might taking a leap of faith work for you now? Where do you need to stop yourself from holding back when your career is concerned?

DEALING WITH DISAPPOINTMENT

As resourceful and quick as you are, there will be times when you feel like you've exhausted all your options. Luckily, there are a few ways to stay positive and motivated when disappointment comes creeping in. As someone who prides yourself on how much you know, it can sometimes be hard to admit when you don't know something. This difficulty can make you incredibly competitive when it comes to how you see yourself compared to others, and you are prone to being too hard on yourself when you feel that you don't match up. While having a competitive spirit isn't a bad thing, you sometimes allow it to get the best of you by taking a setback as a failure on your part. As a result, you'll find yourself overanalyzing everything you think you did, or worse: blowing off your responsibilities or aspirations out of a fear of failure. This is where you need to take a step back and give yourself the space to see the bigger picture. Make note of the things that you did well, which includes giving yourself credit for trying in the first place. Plus, a "loss" doesn't have to be a bad thing. Sometimes not succeeding in getting something means that it isn't the right fit for you.

As an adaptable zodiac sign, you should know more than anyone that you always have options and that losing one option doesn't mean all options are lost. Nor does it mean that you are a failure. Speaking of "failure," do be mindful of allowing others to project their expectations onto you. As a Gemini, you can be surprisingly sensitive about your image and how others see you. When others project their version of success onto you, it keeps you from doing what truly resonates with you out of a desire to live up to their demands. Above all, you must learn how to live life by your own values and rules rather than the values of your family, friends, or others. By trying to be everything to everyone, you only end up losing yourself. This is not to say that you can't be open to the advice of others or that you have to take your rebellious nature to the extreme. It just means that what you want and what makes you happy have value. When you pursue the things and experiences that make you happy, you are performing an act of self-love.

YOUR APPROACH TO WELLNESS

Speaking of self-love, as a sign associated with communication, ideas, and the rational mind, it's important for you to have regular activities and outlets that feed your curiosity and your sense of fun. Whether it's keeping company with a gaggle of friends or flying off on your own solo jaunt, you're at your best when you have the freedom to do as you please and have multiple options at your disposal. But before you dash off, let's explore how you can create the perfect home base to keep you calm and cool.

MAKING YOUR HOME YOUR CASTLE

As busy as your schedule is, you need a home base that helps you unwind and clear your head, as well as get grounded—especially during the times when things get super hectic. Here are a few things to make sure your home is the solid rock you need:

- A minimalist approach to decorating. Keep your space free of clutter to avoid feeling overwhelmed by "stuff," and to keep the energy in your home from getting stagnant. Seek out furniture with clean lines.
- Décor with geometric patterns that speak to your analytical mind.
- Earth tones, including creams and whites, to assist with relaxation.
- A well-stocked home library filled with material showcasing your knowledge and varied interests that you can get lost in.
- A designated space (not your bedroom!) for your gadgets, including your laptop and TV. This helps ensure a more restful sleep.
- A set routine for when you go to bed, eat dinner, etc., to help bring some grounding energy to your day.

GETTING FRESH AIR: TIPS FOR HELPING YOU FEEL RENEWED

When you're feeling stuck, uninspired, or bogged down with one too many things (like responsibility), you can lose the energy that makes you so bubbly in the first place. While the perfect home base will help reenergize you, there are a few other ways to give yourself a reboot.

Get Hands-On

Since Gemini is astrologically in charge of learning, as well as the hands and the nervous system, taking a class where you can learn something hands-on not only stimulates your creativity and feeds your brain but also helps to alleviate anxiety that may be connected to your tendency to overthink.

Get Out Into the Air

Gemini is also in charge of the lungs. This is why techniques that focus on slowing the breath are helpful for you, as is getting actual fresh air. Even better if it's an activity that allows you to feel the sensation of wind blowing over your body, the way you would with a bike ride or when taking a stroll through a park on a breezy day.

Switch Up Your Routines

As a Gemini, you get a bad rap for needing so much variety in your routine, but that variety is integral to your happiness. When you feel like your days have become a little too monotonous and you're getting that itch for something new, making some minor switches in your routines can make a big difference. Making a minor change, like choosing a different place to take your lunch break or taking a different route home from work, can give you a moment of refreshment.

Play a Game

Whether it's a board or video game, a crossword puzzle, or something competitive like poker, pursue activities that appeal to your need for fun, strategy, and outwitting someone else. Get your game on when you want to feel like a kid again.

Write

As a connoisseur of words, writing is to you what air is...well, to you—after all, you are an air sign. When you're feeling blocked and you have a hundred thoughts swirling about in your head, writing is a powerful tool for clearing your mind and seeing things in a different light.

Don't worry about it making sense; the point is to just get everything out and onto paper.

KEEPING IT EASY-BREEZY: TIPS FOR RELIEVING STRESS

Now that you know what to do to get back into the swing of things, let's take a look at what to do when it feels like that swing is swinging out of control. As a sign that lives in your head, processing every little piece of information that comes through, you can suffer from anxiety, irritability, and insomnia when you don't give your mind a chance to rest. The following are a few tips on how to slow down and refocus.

Take a Media Cleanse

In a time when the twenty-four-hour news cycle is a staple to our everyday routines, it is all too easy to overload on information, especially when it comes to bad or disturbing news. As someone who tends to be plugged in and on the pulse of events as they happen, it's important that you give yourself frequent breaks. Studies show that a heavy consumption of news and social media can cause anxiety, depression, and stress. It's no surprise: what we consume daily informs and shapes our lives. As a sign that thrives on information, you need to be mindful of what you "feed" yourself on a regular basis.

Be Mindful of the Company You Keep

Similar to taking a media detox, it is necessary to occasionally reevaluate your social circle too. While gossip can be hard to resist, be wary of people who only have negative things to say, whether they're talking about their own lives or talking about other people. Their energy can have a toxic, draining effect on you.

Get Into Your Heart Space

Being an air sign, you're not usually comfortable with the touchy-feely, mushy stuff, which means that all too often you can get trapped in your head, disconnecting yourself with how you feel. Your feelings are good indicators as to whether you're taking on an obligation out of guilt or to solely please others. For example, are you locking yourself into a meeting or a date because you want to, or are you saying yes to make someone else happy? You can save yourself a lot of stress and discomfort by being 100 percent honest with yourself (and others) about what you can and can't do when it comes to how you spend your time and energy.

Purge

Being a sign that picks up information and outside stimuli at the drop of a hat, you need to keep not only your "psychic" (mental cache) free and clear but also need to do the same with your environment. When old energy is stuck in a room or office, the area can feel heavy or stale. A good way to refresh your space is keeping dirt and clutter down to a minimum, as they hold negative vibes.

CHAPTER 4
CANCER: JUNE 21–JULY 22

Fiercely loving and deeply giving, you teach the rest of the zodiac how to wear their hearts on their sleeves without fear or remorse. Using your gifts of intuition and emotional sensitivity, you can see into the depths of someone's heart and know exactly what they're all about—which is why there's very little that gets past you. Not one to take feelings lightly, you go to great lengths to care for those around you, especially the people you love. When it comes to maintaining your own happiness, it's no surprise then that you need to receive the same love and nurturing that you so readily give. When you don't receive the care you need, you can be left feeling depleted and insecure about your worth.

This chapter is dedicated to helping you learn how to better meet your own needs while still establishing relationships that keep your heart open and your soul full. Not only will you find tips on getting the best out of love and relationships, but you'll also find a guide to wellness and important self-care activities that will bring the best out of you.

MOON CHILD

The Moon has a special place in astrology. Connected with the archetype of the mother, the Moon holds the craving for all things nurturing and nourishing. In many ways, the Moon represents the heart: holding memories, feelings, and deep, soul-felt connections to others. As the sign associated with the Moon, you, too, are like a heart. Prioritizing relationships with others, you can be found at the center of a community or family (much like a heartbeat), running the show with your own brand of strength, support, and tender care.

Defined by the element of water, you live in the realm of feelings and intuition. In fact, these are your superpowers. Like the primordial gods and goddesses that came before you, you possess the power to plug into the pulse of the collective, moving souls and setting trends with your emotional honesty, genuine compassion for others, and old-soul wisdom. Think Nelson Mandela and Princess Diana. While you may get pegged as being overly moody, your many moods are really your way of assessing a person, situation, or experience and adjusting accordingly to match your surroundings—kind of like a chameleon. Your feelings act as your guideposts, helping you to react to situations accordingly, whether it's through kindness and nurture or through your tough, protective shell. Depending on how you feel about a person or situation, it can take a long time to get past that shell. It's not necessarily that you're shy; you just need to feel things out before you feel comfortable (or safe) enough to be seen for your true self.

Once you do let your guard down for someone, you remain loyal and loving to them. This is a big reason why you are celebrated for your nurturing spirit: when you give, you give with very few limits. However, as a sign motivated by emotional security, it is incredibly hurtful for you when you feel that the loyalty and kindness you show others isn't reciprocated.

As a Cancer, you thrive on the support of family and community, just as they thrive on you and your support. This can make you prone to overidentifying with your family or community, as you take on their problems, feelings, or attitudes as if they were your own, losing yourself in the process. As a Cancer, you must learn how to be okay with putting yourself and your needs first at times (sans guilt), as well as how to develop a sense of self that exists outside of the identity of your clan.

Still, few know how to do intimacy quite like you. In fact, when it comes to love and devotion it's easy to see why you leave folks wanting more.

YOUR APPROACH TO LOVE

Like singer and celebrity chef Kelis, who has her Mars (the planet in charge of passion and self-confidence) in Cancer, you tend to bring your admirers to the yard with your milk shake (no, an actual milk shake) and a fresh batch of homemade chocolate-chip cookies. An intuitive and doting partner, you know how to make your beloved feel at home with your affection, home-cooked meals, and family values. This is why you need someone who is as emotionally intelligent as you are—a person who can give you the tenderness and intimacy you need, but can also bring you out of your protective shell or a bad mood. If home is where the heart is, then your love is like a multimillion-dollar mansion.

WOWING WITH COLOR

But your sweet personality isn't the only way you can reel in a love interest. As a sign in tune with feelings and thus passion, you can be quite seductive given the right tools. Although some people will refer to you as being shy, part of your allure is your ability to operate from behind the scenes and maintain an air of mystery. This is why the colors that you wear can speak for you and help you to attract a partner without you having to put yourself on the spot. Here are the colors that best highlight your intuitive and tenderhearted spirit.

Blue-Green

Colors that represent your element (water), like seafoam or aqua green, help boost your mood and make you feel good in your skin, allowing your true magnetism to shine through.

Silver

Much like the Moon, silver reflects light, which can be as eye-catching as it is seductive. Adorning yourself with silver jewelry helps you make an impression. Similar colors like shades of gray also make a bold statement while still allowing you to maintain your mystery—like the Moon.

White

Representing peace and purity, white is a power color for you, as it relates to your compassionate and soulful nature. Depending on how you wear it (a stylish trench coat or a chic fuzzy sweater), it is also a standard of sophistication.

SCENTS FOR POWER AND SEDUCTION

Just as enchanting as color, scent can be used to attract admirers. Ever notice how the power of a scent can evoke a loving memory or a nostalgic feeling? You can use the power of scent to leave the object of your affection with that loving feeling too. The scents that amplify your special gifts also make a strong impression without being overpowering. These are your go-to fragrance families:

Gourmand

Sweet and hard to resist: fragrances that contain these notes tend to attract people to you like bees to honey. Wear these scents and you'll have your admirers hot on your trail in no time. You can also use these scents to boost your mood when in need of a little pick-me-up:

- Brown Sugar
- Candy
- Sugarplum
- Toffee

Soft Floral

Soft floral notes evoke the gentle, tender vibes that you exude. When you're in the spirit to seduce, grab a fragrance that features these scents to set a romantic mood while luring in the one you have your eyes on. These notes can also provide a soothing balm during times of sadness or heartbreak:

- Iris
- Pear Blossom
- Violet
- Water Lily

White Floral

White floral scents have been described as intoxicating, unforgettable, and lush. Fragrances that contain these notes are perfect for the classy dame that you are. Wear these when you want to feel sexy and powerful in your skin:

- Honeysuckle
- Jasmine
- Lily
- White Poppy

DAILY AFFIRMATIONS FOR LOVE

Since you're on the subject of feeling sexy and powerful, another way you can achieve the confidence you need to attract a happy and healthy relationship is through affirmations. Affirmations that you recite to yourself in moments of self-doubt or sadness help to keep you feeling positive and open to the love opportunities waiting for you.

While you long for a forever kind of love affair, it is hard to let go of the past if you've been hurt before. The result? Your past ends up setting the tone for your romantic future, especially if you haven't fully let go of an ex. The following affirmations will help to bring you back into the present, so you can focus on what you want moving forward—instead of what you wanted in the past. As you say them aloud to yourself, practice putting feeling into each one. For example, how would you feel if the perfect mate for you were standing right in front of you? How would this person make you feel regularly? Use those feelings to strengthen these affirmations:

- Love is always available to me, with or without a partner.
- The right relationship for me offers me stability and mutual support.
- My perfect match gives me the intimacy and affection I need.
- The right match for me is someone with whom I can build a home and a family.
- My partner shares my values and is someone with integrity.
- The perfect partner for me appreciates my vulnerability and respects how I feel.
- My partner is sexually compatible with me and keeps the sex interesting and engaging.

DEALING WITH HEARTBREAK AND BREAKUPS

Despite your best efforts, heartbreak and breakups can be an inevitable part of life. But not to worry— there are ways to make sure a heartbreak doesn't have a negative impact on the future of your love life.

In astrology, the element of water is said to hold memories. This is why water signs like you tend to hold on to the past. Thus, you may find yourself pining over your ex and losing yourself in the nostalgia of the past relationship. While you want to move on quickly from heartbreak, trying to force yourself to get over someone quickly can do more harm than good. As an emotional water sign, ignoring or repressing your feelings means that they'll end up spilling out elsewhere, more often in a jarring or misdirected way—like taking your frustration out on others.

The best thing you can do after a breakup is to give yourself space to feel all the emotions as they come. But don't stew in them: allow those feelings to flow through you, cleansing and healing you as you release them. One way you can do this is by writing down how you feel on a few sheets of paper and then burning the paper as a way to release the hurt. Another thing that you can do is become more aware of the thoughts and words you use to speak about your feelings and the breakup. Be honest about naming what you feel—sadness, anger, fear, etc. But try to steer clear of putting yourself down or using words that affirm the negative ("No one will ever love me," "I'll never be happy again," etc.). These statements are untrue and they only make you feel worse. This is why it's important to maintain perspective. Getting your heart broken shouldn't turn you hardened and cold or afraid to love, but it should show you what you can do better for yourself in the future. These lessons will also come in handy in your relationships with family members and friends, especially that important practice of setting boundaries.

HANDLING RELATIONSHIPS WITH FAMILY AND FRIENDS

Since Cancer rules over the areas of home and family, you thrive on the deep, personal ties that you share with your loved ones. These bonds give you a solid sense of security—the security of knowing that you are safe, protected, and have a place to belong. In fact, your need to belong is a big driving force when it comes to how you approach your relationships. Ultimately, your connections to your family and friends are like a lifeline to you: they keep you feeling strong and supported in the face of uncertainty, loss, and whatever else life might toss your way. At the same time, you are also a lifeline to the ones whom you love, and rarely is there a time when you aren't available to offer a loved one an empathetic ear, a hot bowl of soup, or a warm hug. As the archetypal mother of the zodiac, you have a genuine need to provide a safe haven to the people around you.

As a water sign, one of the major things that you tend to struggle with when it comes to your relationships is learning how and when to set boundaries. In astrology, the element of water is considered highly malleable, absorbing the moods, thoughts, and influences of others. As a Cancer, you easily absorb other people's feelings of lack (lack of nurture, lack of nourishment, lack of love, etc.), which in turn incites you to take on the role of fulfilling their needs. Without setting healthy boundaries or limits on how much you give and when, you will be left feeling emotionally drained, resentful, and underappreciated. An important part of setting boundaries means recognizing that you don't always need to have all the answers to everyone's problems. Self-preservation enables you to make sure that there's still enough of you left when all is said and done. Setting boundaries will also help you to weed out flimsy, unsubstantial relationships that take advantage of your kindness and care, freeing you up for relationships that *will* reciprocate your care.

Don't interpret your kindness and care as a hindrance, however. This compassion is what makes the world a better place, and you'll find yourself making a true difference because of it, in your personal life and your career path too.

YOUR APPROACH TO CAREER

Contrary to popular belief, you can be quite the go-getter. As a cardinal sign of the zodiac (*cardinal* means self-motivated), you're at your best when you're initiating ideas and actions, following through on a hunch, or calling the shots in a position that allows you to run the show—especially if the position is behind the scenes. Some of these positions include being an executive chef at a five-star restaurant, a head nurse running an intensive care unit, or a senior officer in the military. Because of your connection to home and family and helping others, you're also drawn to fields like hospitality, social work, and education. Overall, you need a career that not only inspires and motivates you but also fills an emotional need to better the lives of others. As a sensitive and empathic water sign, you need a work environment that feels warm and welcoming, even if the work you do is challenging. Otherwise, you'll frequently find yourself in a bad mood or feeling stuck and energetically wiped out.

DAILY AFFIRMATIONS TO HELP YOU GET AHEAD

So how do you reduce the chances of ending up or staying stuck in a job that you hate? One great way to do so is by using the power of affirmations. Daily affirmations are a great tool in helping you to stay the course toward your dreams. These motivational phrases not only ensure that you are putting out the positive vibes that will draw opportunities to you, but also remind you of things to recall when taking on a new job, working toward a promotion, or reconsidering your current position.

Although you're self-motivated, you can fall victim to periods of inaction and discouragement when you feel like your career isn't moving in the way that you want. This can manifest as chronic complaining about your job or creating dramas in your head about others being out to get you. To avoid this kind of negative thinking, use the following affirmations to assist you in taking action and creating the kind of professional life that you want.

- I believe in myself and possess the confidence to go after my goals and ambitions.
- My career is emotionally rewarding; I regularly feel good about what I do.
- I go above and beyond for my job. I am celebrated for my hard work. I am a true standout and an innovator.
- I get along well with the people I work with; it feels like a close-knit team. I know how to bring out the best in others.
- The perfect job for me provides me with abundance and financial security. I have more than enough.
- I trust my intuition and use it to find the opportunities I seek.
- The perfect job for me allows me to utilize and hone my creative gifts.
- I don't take anything personally; what other people say or do is not a reflection on me.

JOURNAL PROMPTS

You can also channel these affirmations into actionable steps toward success through prompting questions. Questions, such as journal prompts, will get you thinking more proactively about what you have done in the past and how to apply those actions to the present and future.

As a nostalgic Cancer, you can sometimes spend too much time living in the past, which makes it hard for you to move forward or to see the possibilities before you. At the same time, you can be great at getting things started, but you let discouragement or negative thinking get in the way of finishing them. Before you know it, you'll have started a string of projects with no sign of completion in sight, leaving you feeling ineffective. The following journal prompts are designed to help you to think more positively and to find your follow-through:

- Think back to something you accomplished: how did it make you feel when you reached the finish line?
- What's a goal you'd like to accomplish? What are some actionable steps you can take today to help you to get closer to achieving that goal?
- In what ways can you bring more structure and organization to your schedule? How might you better prioritize your to-do list?

DEALING WITH DISAPPOINTMENT

Okay, so what happens when you try your best and follow through on your plans and still come up empty? Disappointments happen. Fortunately, there are ways to deal with these blows and keep on going.

There's a reason why you are associated with a sea creature that carries a tough outer shell—a.k.a. the crab—you are fiercely protective, not just of those you love but of yourself as well. As a result, you are prone to being overly sensitive. While you are incredibly intuitive, you have to be able to figure out if what you feel is really your intuition or if it is your feelings getting the better of you. Maintaining perspective is key, especially when it comes to dealing with disappointment. Perspective asks that you remove your feelings from the equation and look at things from a more rational place. Instead of taking a disappointment, like a slow job search or a project falling through, as an affront to you or your capabilities, consider that sometimes things that happen (or don't happen) have nothing to do with you at all. There are a myriad of things going on with a situation or another person that you aren't privy to. Maybe a slow job search doesn't mean that you aren't qualified; it could mean a slowdown in the market or a surplus of candidates all equally qualified.

Perspective can also help you to tap into the power of acceptance. By accepting a disappointing situation for what it is, you avoid the trouble of inferring inaccurate information or making assumptions based on what isn't. This can spare you from holding on to bitterness or pointing fingers at others. By opening yourself up to all the possibilities and accepting what happens, you give yourself the freedom to let go and move on.

YOUR APPROACH TO WELLNESS

Cultivating success and happiness is about advancing in your career, but also, maybe more so, it is about practicing personal well-being. After all, a healthy you is a happy you.

Being a water sign means that you need lots of alone time to rest and recharge your batteries. As someone who spends so much time looking after and caring for others, you need activities and wellness routines that help you to give back to yourself. Without this self-care, you can become moody and even develop physical health issues such as weight gain, digestive issues, and sluggishness. On your road to wellness, it's important to create a home space that provides you with a rejuvenating pit stop along the way.

MAKING YOUR HOME YOUR CASTLE

Your home is your sanctuary. It's where you go when you need to cocoon yourself away from the noise, crowds, and anything else that keeps you from relaxing your senses. You need a home space that not only offers you a soft place to land but also a space that is visually welcoming. Here are a few items for meeting those needs:

- Aromatic and visually vibrant flowers like jasmine, roses, or stargazer lilies, which create a peaceful vibe while also uplifting your mood.
- Soft lighting in areas like your bedroom or other spaces where you tend to unwind, to create an intimate, cocoon-like atmosphere.
- Subdued colors like light pinks, creams, and neutrals that calm you. Using pink in your home can be especially helpful for healing heartbreak and opening up the heart, as pink is related to unconditional love, compassion, and nurturing.
- Scented candles and diffusers that feature fragrances such as sage, lavender, rose, and frankincense. These scents help to clear out negative energy and lift sadness and bad moods.
- Crystal, mirrored, and glittery accents that reflect light and brighten up the space while adding a touch of luxury.
- Doubles and matching pairs (e.g., matching lamps on either side of your bed). This helps to attract love while also maintaining balance in your home.
- Lots of pillows to create a warm, cozy feel in your space.
- Soothing music or earplugs to block out noise and create a peaceful ambiance.

GETTING FRESH WATER: TIPS FOR FINDING YOUR FLOW

Unfortunately, regardless of your preparations and home escape, there comes a moment (or several) in everyone's life when they feel like they've lost their flow. Should this happen to you, don't worry. There are easy ways to get it back.

Self-care is paramount to your well-being as a Cancer because you spend so much time caring for and doting on others. Since it's so easy to put the needs of others before your own, you need to be a little more uncompromising about setting aside time for yourself and your own needs. If you don't, then you risk losing the energy, confidence, and compassion that make you who you are. Use the following tips to help you with finding your flow and getting back on track.

Take a Bath

As a water sign, it's necessary for you to frequently be in or near water, as it helps to refresh you and cleanse you of stuck or negative energy—especially the energy you may unwittingly absorb from other people. Bathing allows you to take advantage of the healing properties of water while creating a sort of protective bubble for yourself.

Step Into the Past

As a sign connected to the past and to tradition, many Cancers are historians of some sort. Whether it's vintage cars, music, or fashion, you take a special interest in the nostalgia, traditions, and magic of generations past. Museum hopping, antique shopping, or kicking back with some classic tunes are all great ways to get back to feeling like yourself again. Sometimes going back can help you to move forward.

Keep a Journal

When you're feeling off-balance, writing down your thoughts in a journal can help you to gain clarity and perspective while also encouraging you to let go of toxic feelings and negative thinking.

Remember to Eat

Living in an on-the-go world, it can be all too easy to skip meals or allow too much time to go in between meals. This can throw you off your health routine, causing mood swings and fatigue. Avoid this by making sure that you carve out time during your day to eat regularly. If possible, keep some healthy snacks on hand to nibble on as you go about your day.

Cuddle Up

Experts say that cuddling (it doesn't have to be with a romantic partner) releases the feel-good hormone oxytocin. This hormone helps to alleviate pain and boost mood levels. As a nurturing Cancer, you are quite the cuddler. If you sleep alone, having a body pillow nearby can help create that cozy feeling.

RIDING THE WAVE: TIPS FOR RELIEVING STRESS

Sometimes, while you may have your flow, things can get a bit overwhelming. Have no fear, dear Cancer. There are ways to ride out that wave of emotion like a surfing pro. As an emotional water sign, your stress often shows up as depression or a strain on the adrenal system, leading to fatigue and a lack of motivation as well as a fear of opening up to new experiences. This means that activities that best help you to relieve tension are those that discourage you from sitting in your feelings for too long. Use the following tips to shift a bad mood, let go of stress, and find inspiration.

Add Some Heat

Eating spicy foods, using essential oils like cinnamon, clove, and ginger, and practicing hot yoga are all great ways to put some pep in your step and clear through stagnant energy. Heat and movement stimulate blood flow, which can contribute to healthier brain function and mental clarity, and an increase in feel-good hormones like endorphins.

Change Your Scenery

As a homebody, you can get stuck at home for days if left alone long enough. While it is good to unwind in the comfort of your own home, seeing the same thing day after day can create a stagnant feeling. Changing your scenery through travel or a simple walk around the block are good ways to refresh your energy. You might even consider booking a room for a night or two at a swanky hotel and enjoying a staycation (a mini vacation away from your home but still within driving distance of where you live).

Find Things That Make You Laugh

In this day of modern technology, it is all too easy to see bad news. This is why it's important to have a balance when it comes to the kind of information that you choose to absorb. Challenge yourself to find at least one thing to make you laugh each day. It can be a silly movie, a joke told by a friend, or something you read. It really doesn't matter what it is as long as it brings a smile to your face.

Get Busy

Sometimes the best way to beat stress or the moody blues is to find a project, like organizing your closet, clearing out your inbox, or completing some other small, manageable task. Doing this won't only help you to clear your head but will also give you a sense of being in control and taking charge of your life.

CHAPTER 5
LEO: JULY 23–AUGUST 22

Possessing a magic and majesty about you that's nearly impossible to duplicate, you approach life with a flair in your step and fire in your heart. Commanding the spotlight wherever you go, you believe life isn't worth living unless you get to be yourself. In fact, it's your self-expressive nature that makes you so inspiring. Others can only dream of being as bold as you, while you have no problem showing up and showing off. Still, you're not just about yourself, as your warmth and generosity toward others are some of your greatest qualities. If someone is in need, you can bet that you're one of the first people to help.

However, as bright as your star is, there are still things that can get in your way and dim your light. That's why you'll find the guidance in this chapter to help you maintain, or reclaim, your shine, from love to personal wellness.

HEY NOW, YOU'RE A ROCK STAR

It's no surprise that some of the biggest celebrity names fall under the zodiac sign of Leo: Jennifer Lopez, Madonna, Viola Davis, and former US president Barack Obama, for starters. That's because when it comes to true star power, Leos like you have the game locked down. As the astrological sign ruled by the brightest, hottest star in our solar system (the Sun), you bring that megawatt power down to Earth with your warmth, generosity, incomparable talent, and killer style. Even if you don't have any plans to work in Hollywood, you are still that one person in the room that makes the rest of us sit up and take notice. Essentially, you were born to stand out. This is because, at your core, you have a desire to express yourself in all your fabulousness—unabashed and unfiltered. In fact, this authentic self-expression is often your driving force. By showing up as you are, you fuel and inspire the rest of us by shining your light with a ferocity and verve that can only warrant the deepest appreciation. You also thrive on that appreciation, seeking out life experiences and everyday connections with others that thrust you into the spotlight to be celebrated and adored.

As a natural-born leader, you gain followers with your fiery spirit, unwavering loyalty, and creative genius. However, when you lose sight of your own specialness by seeing yourself through another's eyes instead of your own, it can dull your shine. For example, when you find yourself doing things solely for attention or applause, like bragging a little too much about yourself or blowing the bank on clothing you can't afford, it's time to take a step back and remember how unique you are outside of the gaze of an audience. This isn't to say that you shouldn't want the steady time and attention of a devoted partner or be the picture of success to your friends. By all means, flaunt what you've got! However, when you become too concerned about what others think about you, you risk losing your authentic self as a result. As a sign that is all about self-expression, you need to live from a self-centered place. No, not in the obnoxious, inconsiderate sense of the word but in the sense of living from your heart. In other words, do things that make you happy regardless of whether people are watching. And that's the thing about being a Leo: recognizing that self-approval isn't so much about competing for attention or boosting your ego at the expense of others. Instead, it's about becoming comfortable in your own skin and living with confidence and integrity, regardless of what others think about you. When you are focusing on being the best you, for you, you attract the kind of good vibes that will make you truly successful in things like love and family relationships.

YOUR APPROACH TO LOVE

Romantic, playful, and oh-so bighearted, you never do anything on a small scale and that includes your love life. Preferring to shower the object of your affection with larger-than-life tokens of love, lavish gifts, expensive trips, and all those gratuitous couple selfies is your modus operandi. Longing to be the better half of a power couple, you approach relationships with a passion and ferocity that lets your partners know you're all in, giving them the pleasure of experiencing your die-hard loyalty and star power. Built for the spotlight and a thousand adoring fans, you're looking for a mate who will be the president of said fan club. This means that praise, appreciation, and a mutual sense of loyalty from your partner is paramount to your happiness in love (and in the bedroom).

There's no denying that you love being noticed when it comes to wooing a crush. With a few extra tricks up your sleeve, you'll be shining that much brighter with minimal effort.

WOWING WITH COLOR

Bold, vibrant colors are a trademark of Leo's sense of style and brand of fashion. But did you know that there are specific colors that best represent and enhance your fiery spirit, warmth, and fun-loving soul? Incorporating these colors as staples into your wardrobe will help you to feel your best and catch the eye of someone special.

Gold

Associated with wealth, luxury, and royalty, gold is the perfect match for a gilded icon like you. Adorning yourself with gold accessories and clothing inspires that connection to prosperity, inviting it into your life (especially if you're looking for a mate who's as generous as they are good-looking and kind). Rose gold is a great option too!

Orange

A color of creativity, joy, and sexual energy, orange not only sends a message to your soon-to-be beloved about just how much fun you are, it also helps you to bounce back from heartbreak or sadness.

Red

This one might be a no-brainer, considering that it's scientifically proven that the color red activates the part of the brain that deals with sex, passion, and hunger. When it comes to love, red is a powerful tool for ramping up the attraction.

Yellow

Like the sun's rays, yellow represents warmth and positive energy as well as mental clarity. Use yellow accents to stimulate good vibes and attract a love that is rooted in joy, optimism, and positive communication. Add pops of yellow into your wardrobe with a cute bag, a pair of flirty sandals, or a sunny nail polish. Of course, you can always go for some dramatic fun with yellow faux fur or a stylish satin dress.

SCENTS FOR POWER AND SEDUCTION

For a showstopper like you, using color to attract love might be a no-brainer—but what about the power of smell? Being the powerhouse that you are, you need scents that fuel your fiery spirit and help you command attention. The following are the fragrance families that will help you to shine your brightest. You can also use these scents to create signature fragrances that are all your own.

Citrus

Fresh and uplifting, this fragrance has a special connection to you, as the Sun, your planetary ruler, is in charge of citrus fruit! Go for perfumes and essential oils that contain these notes when you want to share your sunshiny spirit with the world:

- Blood Orange
- Neroli
- Passion Fruit
- Yuzu

Spicy

Warm and invigorating, much like you, spicy fragrances like these are great for turning up the heat and turning on the passion. Go for these notes when you want to stir up a little drama and a whole lot of fun:

- Bay Leaf
- Cinnamon
- Clove
- Saffron

Floral

Lush and delicious, floral notes make for fragrances that linger and leave a lasting impression, just like you. Wear fragrances that contain these floral scents when you want to remind folks why you're a true standout:

- Chamomile
- Heliotrope
- Mimosa
- Ylang-Ylang

DAILY AFFIRMATIONS FOR LOVE

As a dynamic fire sign, part of your success in love is also in affirming and asserting yourself through your experiences and your approach to life. Daily affirmations are a great way to pull love into your orbit. Affirmations also serve as a reminder of the things that you need in a relationship and romantic partner in order to truly flourish.

As fiery and fabulous as you are, you deserve someone who can hold their own and match you toe-to-toe—in their own life as well as a life they share with you. Nevertheless, out of a desire for adoration, you sometimes settle for partners who can talk a good game with lots of flash and drama but do little to back it up. On another note, your thirst for success can also push you to become domineering and demanding, especially when you don't get your way. This leads you to attract significant others with whom power struggles and control issues are a norm. Use the following affirmations to help you attract mates of a higher caliber: people who will not only treat you like royalty but who will also be regal in their own right. At the same time, look to these affirmations when you need to be reminded of how special and worthy you are, so you don't settle for less or betray what your heart really wants.

- I radiate light and beauty wherever I go; I attract love with ease.
- The right relationship for me is filled with passion, playtime, and creativity.
- The perfect match for me is my true partner and equal.
- The perfect match for me showers me with romance and attention.
- My partner adores me and makes me feel like royalty.
- I am smart and worthy enough to not settle for less than what I deserve from love.
- The right relationship for me is based on loyalty and trust.

- When I am in the company of my partner, I feel confident and supported.

DEALING WITH HEARTBREAK AND BREAKUPS

Despite your positive vibes and assertive attitude, there will be times when love isn't so bright and sunny. Luckily, there are simple things you can do to come out of these setbacks with your fiery spirit still blazing.

As a die-hard romantic and fixed fire sign, you don't get over your break-ups as easily as your fellow fire signs, Aries and Sagittarius. That's because when you love, you love fast and fierce. You are also prone to giving your power away to an undeserving partner in exchange for the feeling of being in control, only to have that person commit the ultimate sin by betraying you with an act of disloyalty or blatant disregard for your feelings. Ouch! This is why the key to moving past a breakup is showering *yourself* with the love and attention you seek rather than looking for it from someone else. When you choose to show yourself regular acts of self-love, it is harder to settle for matches that are nowhere in your league. At the same time, the act of self-love also sends out a vibe that you recognize your worth, helping you to attract mates of a higher caliber. Another key to breaking the pattern of less deserving love interests is to give your significant others space to prove their worthiness to you. This means not just going by their words but paying close attention to their actions too. Empty gestures, a flashy personality, and lip service are not enough.

Still, heartbreak is sometimes inevitable, and you will find it difficult to let go of the relationship depending on how badly you were hurt. The best thing you can do when dealing with heartbreak is give yourself space to heal and nurse your wounds. Don't be shy about leaning on your friends for support either. Being a Leo, you put a lot of pressure on yourself to be fearless and invulnerable and to always keep a sunny disposition. If there's one thing that you hate, it is to be embarrassed or sunken deep down into your feelings with a case of the blues. However, you have to learn to let go of the need to stay in control. Your authenticity through thick *and* through thin is what makes you so endearing and loveable in the first place. Honor the genuine you, and you'll find it easier to establish true connections with others (including love interests) who honor it too.

HANDLING RELATIONSHIPS WITH FAMILY AND FRIENDS

As a fire sign ruled by the Sun, your warmth and generosity are just two of the many reasons why you are so loved by your friends and family. Another reason is your unwavering loyalty; just as you stick by your partners through thick and through thin, you stick by your friends and family too. You also expect that they show you the same loyalty in return and are left incredibly hurt when this doesn't happen the way you want it to. This can earn you the status of being bossy. Ultimately, you need to learn how to give people the space to show up for you rather than assume they won't, feeding your fear. At the same time, just as with potential mates, it's important for you to pay attention to who does show up and when and to establish a healthy give-and-take between you and the people you love. When you set appropriate boundaries between yourself and others, you lessen the chances of being used for your generosity and unwavering loyalty, and you also learn how to not give up everything you have to others. This may mean cutting off an unhealthy friendship or minimizing the space that an overbearing parent has in your life.

Similar to your approach to romantic partners is your struggle with vul-nerability in relationships with friends and family. As a Leo, you take pride in showing others how self-reliant and confident you are, but it's your vulnerability—your ability to ask for help and to show your less courageous side—that makes you relatable to your loved ones. Does this mean that you have to deny what makes you special? Not at all. It merely means that it's okay to take time off from carrying the weight of the world on your shoulders sometimes.

At the same time, expressing your vulnerability with others may also require the ability to recognize when you are wrong and the ability to apologize and make amends. If you always have to be in the right (a need that stubborn Leos are prone to), how do you have relationships with others that are healthy and balanced? How will you be able to learn from others or develop a sense of mutual respect? Being in the wrong doesn't mean that you're a bad person or even a dumb person. It just means that you need to consider someone else's feelings or point of view from time to time. By respecting others and validating their feelings, you keep your relationships and your sense of community strong. Keeping these habits strong, believe it or not, will lend strength to all aspects of your life, including your career path.

YOUR APPROACH TO CAREER

The love of the good life doesn't only fuel your romances, it extends to your professional life too. Choosing jobs where following your heart is a prerequisite, you need a career that offers you the platform to show off your creative talents while providing you with plenty of autonomy as well (after all, a sign associated with the top of the food chain doesn't fancy being told what to do). Of course, a lion's share of money is always a draw too—you need to be able to fund those big-ticket purchases you love, like that three-week vacation to Dubai or that fourth pair of Louboutin shoes. This is why you can be found in supervisory roles or careers that require an artistic acumen, like acting, deejaying, or designing fashion.

Whatever you choose to do for a living, it has to feed your passion and give you the space to shine. Being stuck in a soul-sucking or overly stressful job will quickly deplete your Leonine energy. The same goes for jobs that leave you feeling undervalued or unappreciated.

DAILY AFFIRMATIONS TO HELP YOU GET AHEAD

Daily affirmations are a great tool in helping you stay the course toward your dreams. These motivational phrases not only ensure that you are putting out the positive vibes that will draw opportunities to you, but also remind you of things to recall when taking on a new job, working toward a promotion, or reconsidering your current position.

As the zodiac sign associated with willpower and strength, you should remember that there's nothing you can't accomplish if your heart is set on it. This sentiment is no different when it comes to your career and your professional goals. Yet as confident as you are, you can still be gripped by feelings of impostor syndrome (that feeling that you don't deserve your success because you're not as good as others think you are) as well as an inability to recognize how much your talent is really worth. The following affirmations are designed to help you through those times when your confidence feels shaky and you need some reassurance when asking for the kind of financial compensation you want:

- I am an intelligent, creative, and unstoppable force. I know my value and pursue opportunities that align with my worth.
- I am worthy of my achievements and my success. I put in the time and dedication to achieve my goals.
- I am capable of getting the job (or client) of my dreams.
- I am financially thriving and my blessings are abundant.

- I am more than what people think of me; I live beyond the approval of others.
- I am becoming better at what I do every day. I am always showing up as the best version of myself.
- I radiate style, charm, and grace. People want to work with me.
- I am a valued and respected member of my field. I possess the integrity and the know-how to get the job done.
- I know that what's meant for me will always find me.
- I am always choosing experiences that allow me to grow, have fun, and feed my passions.

JOURNAL PROMPTS

You can move things a step further by using prompting questions to explore how you can take some of the challenges you may be facing in your career and turn them into opportunities for growth.

Being a fiery Leo, your passion and determination are keys to helping you see your goals through. However, when the going gets tough or you've faced a major setback, it helps to have a little reminder handy to remember how much of a powerhouse you are. By that same token, it's also important to remember that you have a community of people behind you that is ready and willing to help you through those challenges. The following journal writing prompts will help you remember your resourcefulness—and your resources:

- When faced with an obstacle, how do you overcome it? Name a time when you faced a challenge and won.
- How can you make the most of your community? Who are some people you can reach out to for help?

- What are you most proud of right now and why? In what ways could you be gentler with yourself about things you aren't as proud of?

DEALING WITH DISAPPOINTMENT

Unfortunately, no matter your preparation, setbacks are often a part of the professional world. No worries! There are ways you can bounce back when your career and your confidence have taken a hit. More so than most, you need to feel valued for what you do. Thus, when faced with a disappointment, it's often because you tried something, it didn't go the way you wanted, and now you're thinking that maybe it's because you aren't good enough. This need for appreciation is linked to your challenges around self-worth. As you beat yourself up for being "inadequate," you seek the validation of others to prove to yourself that you are wrong. As mentioned before in this chapter, you may even suffer from impostor syndrome: that feeling that you don't deserve a promotion, salary raise, etc., because your struggle with self-worth has you thinking that you're a fraud. In trying to deal with or stave off disappointment, you can end up going overboard trying to show your value to others. The real lesson here is learning how to see this value yourself. Having physical reminders of your accomplishments or daily mantras that help you to affirm and internalize your value will help you in overcoming this challenge.

You might also find yourself dealing with disappointment when you feel like the work that you've put into your career isn't paying off financially. In this case, you wonder, "What's the point?" or, "Why them and not me?" If you do find yourself feeling this way, ask yourself if what you're pursuing is something that you're really invested in. Although financial security is important, your career should be about your passions first and about money second. And when it does come down to money, it is important that you are getting what you're worth and not settling for less. As a Leo, you can be quite generous with your time, energy, and expertise, but if you struggle with self-worth, you can find yourself settling for jobs that are long on hours and short on cash. Recognize that you bring something to the table that's worth the extra bucks in the bank. One way to see your value in a less biased light is to take a break from social media. When you see only the picture-perfect parts of others' lives, it is easy to forget that they, too, deal with setbacks and disappointment, and you may feel bad about yourself as a result. Fortunately, there are easy ways to get back into a place of good feelings about your situation and yourself.

YOUR APPROACH TO WELLNESS

As an energetic fire sign, you thrive on fun—so much so, that it's no coincidence your sign is associated with children, childlike play, and creativity. This means that when it comes to taking care of yourself and doing things that feel good to you, you seek out activities and experiences that allow you to tap into that playful, creative energy. This may be by way of a hobby like dancing or singing or some form of artistry that allows you to express yourself in front of a captive audience. Your source of fun can also be as simple as getting together with friends for a game night—though you'd never say no to a trip to Las Vegas.

MAKING YOUR HOME YOUR CASTLE

But before you hop on that plane, make sure you've got a solid home base to return to. With just a few essentials, you'll have the personal space you need for reenergizing your batteries. As an outgoing fire sign, you expend much of your energy conquering the world and seizing the day with your many plans and projects. This means that you need a stable home base—or lion's den—that allows you to recharge in style, comfort, and lots of privacy. Here are a few things to ensure that your home is "up to code":

- Orange, red, or yellow accents, such as artwork, to uplift your mood.
- Curtains that filter in natural lighting and also block out the light when you're in need of rest and solitude.
- Deep purples or blues in areas where you sleep or relax to create a lounge-y, intimate vibe.
- Scented candles and essential oils that feature musky, calming scents like patchouli, vanilla, or sandalwood.
- A designated space away from others where you can have some peace and solitude.
- Plush carpeting and bedding that will make you feel like royalty.
- Noise-canceling earplugs or a white noise app to help create a quieter atmosphere, especially if you share space with other people.

REKINDLING THE FIRE: TIPS FOR RECLAIMING YOUR SPARK

Now that you are feeling more comfortable in your home, it's time to feel more comfortable in your mind, body, and soul. Luckily, there are simple ways you can reclaim your spark in no time.

You may have experienced this before: that moment or series of moments when you feel like you've lost all your luster. Maybe you find you aren't as interested in dressing up or styling your hair. Maybe you feel weighed down with responsibility and can't remember the last time you just let yourself have some fun, or maybe you're stuck in a rut and you've lost your zest for life. Here are a few easy tips for re-stoking your fire:

Get Some Sunlight

Much like your planetary ruler, the Sun, that warms and nourishes the Earth, you have an inner flame that not only keeps you going but keeps others going as well. When things get stressful, it can be easy to lose your connection to that passionate energy. This is why taking in some sun on a regular basis helps to shift your mood. Plus, sunlight promotes vitamin D production in the body, which can guard against inflammation and high blood pressure. As the sign associated with the heart and circulatory system, this is especially beneficial for you. The Sun is your cosmic battery, ready to recharge and energize you as needed.

Get Your Body Moving

As a dynamic fire sign, you need healthy ways in which you can burn off or channel your excess energy. Sitting still for long periods of time can negatively affect your buoyant, playful mood. You're all about fun and playtime, which means that jogging in place on a treadmill or doing a bunch of sit-ups won't be your speed. That's why cardio-based exercises like Zumba or roller skating can give you the juice you need, while pole dancing or an equally sexy dance-based workout lets you feel like the star you are. You can also try weight lifting, as the act of putting your muscles to the test will make you feel like a superhero.

Hit the Karaoke Bar

There's something about a lion's roar that puts everyone on notice. A roar is affirming: it says, "I'm in my zone, don't mess with me!" And as a Leo, you sometimes have to remind yourself of just how fierce you really are. Belting out one of your favorite songs under neon lights, with your best friends cheering you on, is the perfect reminder. But you don't have to leave your house to release your roar. Next time you're alone, cue up a badass song from your playlist and sing along in front of the mirror. Bonus points if you play a little dress-up while you do it! Impromptu selfie shoot, anyone?

Invite Your Inner Child on a Playdate

Ah, the simplicity of childhood. Remember what it was like to be carefree, innocent, and a die-hard fan of Saturday morning cartoons? Well, it doesn't hurt to have a little reminder from time to time. Pick something that brings out the big kid in you and make it a date. You can bring someone along with you, but this should be something that you do for yourself and yourself alone. It could be going to see the latest animated movie, hitting up an old-school arcade, or attending a comic book convention. Go-karting and playing kickball are great options too. Whatever brings a smile to your face and laughter into your heart—do it. The point is to get out and leave all the adulting behind for a little while.

Try Something You've Never Done Before

As a fixed sign (a.k.a. someone who's not exactly comfortable with change), you risk falling into the kind of rut that dampens your spirits and robs you of inspiration. Pushing yourself to frequently try new things is not only good for jump-starting your confidence and fearless attitude, but also for opening yourself up to new experiences that will get your creative juices flowing and your unique fire burning.

However, what happens when things get a little too hot to handle? Stress. Not to worry; there are easy ways to keep cool.

KEEPING COOL UNDER FIRE: TIPS FOR RELIEVING STRESS

You know what it feels like when things are stuck or stagnant. And you also know what it feels like when things seem like they're spinning out of control: you feel pressed for time, overworked, and like there's a crisis to handle at every turn. The following are ways that you can cool down so you can get back to doing what you love: having a good time.

Stick to a Schedule

As the sign associated with playtime and creativity, you are prone to overindulging in activities that keep you up and out at all hours of the night (like excessive partying) as well as in foods and drinks that aren't good for you. This is where exercising some self-discipline comes in handy: try cutting back on something in your diet (like sugar), being pickier about the social obligations you agree to, or sticking to a more consistent sleep schedule.

Cool Off with a Meditation

In astrology, Leo is in charge of the heart and circulatory system, which means hypertension can become an issue for you when stress is left unchecked—especially since you tend to hold on to anger and resentment. As a fire sign, you need stress relievers that bring some cooling energy to the table to help you to stay balanced. In Ayurvedic yoga, there's a breathing technique known as the *cooling breath*. This technique is helpful for cooling down the mind and the body—virtually anywhere. Start by drawing your attention inward and being mindful about your breathing. Then, curl your tongue upward toward the roof of your mouth, breathing through your mouth on inhalation and through your nose on exhalation. Repeat these steps until you feel a difference in your body and energy. You should feel calmer, cooler, and relaxed.

Do Something You've Been Putting Off

Tending to the small, everyday, mundane stuff, like cleaning the house or keeping your files organized, is not something you tend to enjoy. You often let things pile up until they hit critical mass and then stress yourself out trying to get everything done in a short window of time. Start your plan of attack by handling the things that you've been dreading doing the most. You can break down the list into smaller steps as well. Try scheduling out blocks of time for things that may take longer to complete, like organizing a closet, doing laundry, or deep cleaning the bathroom, instead of trying to attack everything at once or on days when you already have more than enough to do. When it comes to getting rid of clutter, you may want to start with the immediate stuff like recycling junk mail or clearing out a junk drawer, and then come back to tossing the larger stuff like old clothes. Completing these less-than-fun tasks will lighten your load and leave you feeling more in control of your busy life.

Create a Cocoon for Yourself

With all the energy that you consume and put out each day, you need to create a time in your schedule to adequately recharge. Taking frequent periods of solitude, away from the spotlight, will allow you to rest and rejuvenate. Whether you cocoon yourself away at home (sans social media) or decide to have yourself a staycation holed up in a hotel room or an Airbnb in a different part of your city, never underestimate the power of a quiet, cozy place. Snuggle up on your couch, keep the lights low, and imagine that you're turning your home space into a womb of sorts. Make it warm, protective, and nourishing.

CHAPTER 6
VIRGO: AUGUST 23–SEPTEMBER 22

Intelligent, resourceful, and possessing the heart of a saint, it's hard to find anything not to like about you. With your ability to improve the lives of others through your astute observations, unwavering support, and willingness to take difficult challenges head-on (like taking care of your sick grandparent while working fifty hours a week and pursuing your second master's degree), you don't just set the bar—you raise it over and over again. Priding yourself on productivity and perfection, you often hold yourself to a higher standard than others—though as unpretentious as you are, no one would notice. To keep excessive worry and self-criticism from getting the best of you, it's necessary for you to learn how to be gentler with yourself and to accept that there are always going to be things in life that are beyond your control.

This chapter is dedicated to providing you with the tools to conquer your self-doubt, be more flexible, and have healthy relationships with significant others, friends, and family. With your track record for rising above and beyond a challenge, you'll be on your path to happiness and success in no time.

YOU'VE GOT THE RIGHT STUFF

There's a saying that goes, "If you want something done right, hire a Virgo." Actually, it's not a real saying—but it should be. As a Virgo, you are known for efficiency, productivity, and finding solutions to the toughest problems, so you always get the job done right. Sharing a planetary ruler (Mercury) with Gemini, you are also blessed with the same sharp mind and ability to think on your feet. Mercury bestows you with the power to break down and process information at lightning speed. However, while Gemini is more concerned with ideas and the immaterial world, you—as an earth sign—take things a step further by focusing on how ideas and information can be skillfully applied to the real world.

As a Virgo, you pride yourself on being useful, and this is one of the things that drives you to help others. Even superstar Virgos like Beyoncé and Michael Jackson have lived their lives in service to others, not only through their inspirational music and performances but also through their philanthropy. This is why you may find yourself in a profession that involves helping others, such as coaching or medicine. Represented in astrology by virginity and purity (a.k.a. the virgin), a Virgo's life mission is to make things better through a process of refinement. Whether it's through fitness and nutrition or by creating the patent for the next life-changing invention, your passion is to show the rest of us what needs improving and how to improve it.

Still, it's important that you are careful of defining your identity solely by how much you do (or don't do). Being your own toughest critic, you tend to push yourself harder and further than most, setting exceptionally high expectations and blaming yourself when things don't go as perfectly as you planned. This is why you are often pegged as a control freak. Your desire to achieve perfection can trump your ability to accept yourself as you are. You must learn to master the art of surrender and acceptance. When you expend your energy trying to control every facet and detail of your life, you become prone to worry and anxiety over all the things that could go wrong. While being practical and prepared is a good thing, so is having faith that things will work out as they should and (even more so) having faith in yourself.

In your relationships, you thrive on helping others and being needed. However, when you base your self-worth on how much you do for others, you end up attracting people who are constantly in need of fixing. As a Virgo, your mission is to develop your powers of discernment to figure out who (and what) deserves your attention and who (and what) doesn't.

YOUR APPROACH TO LOVE

Being as smart and resourceful as you are, it's no surprise that one of the things that appeals to you about being in a relationship is the joy of learning new things with (and from) your partner. In short, you're attracted to brains as well as beauty; but hold the pretense please: you're no snob. You're far too kindhearted and down-to-earth. In fact, you can spot arrogance and inauthenticity a mile away, and it quickly turns you off. Some may call you picky when it comes to choosing a mate, but it's not that—you simply want the best that life has to offer, and that includes romantic partners. The person who wins your heart will be someone who recognizes that being with you is a step up from what they may have had in the past. Cue Beyoncé's "Upgrade U."

WOWING WITH COLOR

Speaking of an upgrade, you can upgrade your seduction game with a little help from the senses! Keep reading, and you'll find the colors that best represent your sharp wit and your polished look. Wear these colors to complement your unique charm.

Dark Green

Deep hues of green work for you because of their connection to stability, ambition, and wealth. Go for a dark green power suit when you're ready to show the world you mean business or a double-breasted wool coat for a chic yet classic look. A green bag or purse works too (it could even help you to attract more money).

Navy Blue

Expertise, authority, substance. These are just a few of the characteristics associated with navy blue. A power color of sorts, this color is a perfect addition to your wardrobe when you want to: 1. feel empowered, and 2. be remembered for the icon that you are.

Brown Earth Tones

With you being an earth sign, this is sort of a no-brainer. Just remember that wearing earth tones doesn't have to be boring. You can use them to elevate a look through opulent textures, like suede, leather, or cashmere, without trying too hard, letting admirers know up front that your beauty comes naturally.

SCENTS FOR POWER AND SEDUCTION

Even though you're an intellectual sign that deals with facts and figures, you're still an earth sign, which means you can be quite sensual too. Did you know you can engage the sense of smell to attract love? As a multitasking maven, you need fragrances that can serve multiple purposes too. The following fragrance families have healing properties as well as fun and feel-good benefits. You can use some of these fragrant notes to attract love, while others can be used to boost your confidence or calm frazzled nerves.

Fruity

Crisp, refreshing—these notes make up fragrances that work well as a pick-me-up and leave you with a fresh, just-showered vibe. In terms of romance and attraction, scents that contain these notes help you be more light and carefree—perfect for date night:

- Cucumber
- Green Apple
- Petitgrain
- Pomelo

Herbal

Since your sign is associated with herbs because of their healing properties, wearing scents that contain these notes will help quiet your busy mind and shift negative thinking that can block love from coming into your life:

- Clary Sage
- Dried Grass
- Tarragon
- Tea
- Wild Grass

Floral

Being an earth sign, you will find that flowers are always going to be your go-to fragrance, as they represent abundance and fertility—just like the virgin. Flowers with fresh, vibrant scents work best for you, as they help you make a powerful statement without coming on too strong. Use these fragrances when you want to tap into your seductive, yet still sweet, side:

- Bamboo
- Orange Blossom
- White Musk
- Wildflower
- Violet Leaf

DAILY AFFIRMATIONS FOR LOVE

You've got your signature colors and seductive scents, but before you waft your orange blossom toward that new crush, there is one more item to add to your arsenal. Words and communication are also a major part of what makes you, as a Virgo, powerful in love. Through daily affirmations, you can use the power of words to boost your love life.

Always ready to provide the backup and support that your partner needs, you are admired by your partners for how devoted you are and for how much you bring to the table. If there's one thing your significant other can count on, it's you. Yet, because you often have a hard time with celebrating your accomplishments and the things about you that make you special, you often grapple with the belief that you aren't worthy of happiness. This shaky sense of self-worth can translate into a desire to be needed and to prove yourself indispensable to the one you love, putting you in situations with romantic partners that require fixing or constant hands-on care, which leaves you feeling more like the help than a true equal.

The love affirmations that follow are geared toward accepting your imperfections and identifying good versus bad love matches, so that you can find a healthy, happy relationship with someone who wants and appreciates you but doesn't necessarily *need* you—someone who is willing to give something worthwhile to you and your union. Wouldn't that be nice for a change?

- I am healthy and whole; I love myself as I am. My partner is healthy and whole too.
- The perfect partner for me showers me with unconditional love.
- The perfect partner for me works to consistently bring their best self to our relationship.
- The right relationship for me provides me with a strong mental and emotional connection to my partner.

- My partner appreciates the value that I bring to their life.
- The perfect relationship for me is sexually satisfying.

DEALING WITH HEARTBREAK AND BREAKUPS

Even with your best foot forward, there may still be times when it is necessary to let a relationship go entirely. Don't fret—there are a few simple ways to recognize when this is the case and to move on with a positive outlook of the future. Recognizing that there's always room for improvement, you have little qualms about pitching in and getting your hands dirty when it comes to maintaining a relationship. Nonetheless, your tendency to give all you've got means that you may find partners who take advantage and who are not always up for helping out, forcing you to pick up the slack. For you, deeply caring for someone means you hold yourself responsible for the things that they do in, and outside of, the relationship. This means that when a breakup does happen, you often take it quite hard, feeling as though you didn't live up to the perfect picture that you envisioned. What you must learn is that there's no such thing as a perfect partner or a perfect relationship. In love, it's about figuring out what works for you and your partner, not sticking to some rigid, cookie-cutter template of how you think things should be. You must determine what's perfect for *you*.

Your relationships with others help to teach you about the power of unconditional love. While there's always room for improvement, it's crucial to be mindful of expecting others to be flawless or of becoming hypercritical and judgmental when a partner falls short. Instead of finger-pointing and playing a blame game, sometimes a breakup can show you where there is more room for personal growth, while allowing others to embody the full range of their own humanness. Mastering the lessons around acceptance also means that when it comes to a breakup and the healing process that follows, it's important for you to be gentle with yourself. Try not to look at a breakup as a failure or as something that you did wrong. Sometimes a relationship is simply not meant to last, and sometimes a partner is unable or unwilling to do their part. In order for a relationship to run smoothly, your partner has to be ready, willing, and able to improve themselves and the relationship. Essentially, you can't be the only one willing to do the work.

Give yourself space to grieve the death of the relationship, but don't use it as a way to tally mistakes and wrongdoings. Instead, push yourself to challenge old beliefs or limiting perceptions about love. Practice forgiveness—of yourself and former partners. Take a sabbatical and travel; clear your head and refresh your energy. Get comfortable with treating yourself well. Above all, be grateful for what you learned as a result of the relationship you were in, and use that information to make improvements in your love life—and your family life—going forward.

HANDLING RELATIONSHIPS WITH FAMILY AND FRIENDS

It may feel like your friends are more your family at times than your actual family, as you may find them to be more understanding than the folks who raised you. As a nurturing Virgo, you're likely to spend your time providing advice and other forms of assistance to help them out of a tight spot or to stay on track. While being there for someone in need is what makes you such a great friend, it's important to be mindful of becoming your friends' life coach or parent. The result is often lopsided friendships where you're left wondering why the only time you hear from them is when they have a problem. In order to prevent this from happening, you have to get used to standing back and allowing your friends to find ways to solve their own problems. This may mean not picking up the phone every time they call or leaving a message unread. By the same token, you have to get comfortable with allowing your friends to show you the same support and dedication that you show them. As a Virgo, you're self-reliant and pride yourself on the number of things that you're able to juggle simultaneously, but you must learn the art of being vulnerable from time to time. Asking for and receiving help is not a sign of weakness or incompetence; in fact, being vulnerable allows you to fully open up to your friends and let them into your deeper thoughts and fears, creating an even stronger bond.

While you share a close bond with your friends, you also have a strong connection to your roots, thanks to the stories and rich history passed down through generations, as well as your family's spiritual beliefs and traditions. Despite this connection, you may be feeling a bit wanting emotionally, as you might have had a parent who was a little too hands-off or who placed a ton of importance on reason over emotion. This may have you thinking it's impossible to let down your guard or blustering through how you feel. Know that you can be up-front and emotionally honest about how you feel while exercising compassion and understanding. At the same time, recognize that your feelings don't have to come in a neat or acceptable package to be valid. Living in your truth can be a messy thing to do. This may require you to speak up more about how you feel when you're dealing with your family, regardless of how they may take it. It may also require recognizing that your family's belief system and your belief system may not align, and that's okay too. At your core, you need the freedom to explore the world around you and to form your own beliefs and values based on your own experiences. Independence doesn't always come easy—sometimes you have to take it. This may mean moving away from home or having a place outside of your home where you can frequently get away. It is also important to accept that the needs and interests that are independent of your family are valid. Validity is also a main theme when it comes to your success in the professional world.

YOUR APPROACH TO CAREER

Ruling the part of the zodiac that involves work, health, and routine, you are drawn to professions that allow you to improve the lives of others. You also push yourself to hone your skills, putting you at the top of your game. These jobs include health-related fields like personal training, physical therapy, nutrition, and surgical medicine. Since you are ruled by Mercury, the planet in charge of communication and discernment, industries associated with writing, journalism, math, and science are also a great fit.

Despite how capable and qualified you are, you must learn to be wary of taking on jobs where you feel undervalued or taken for granted. This is because of your tendency to undersell and downplay your skills and achievements. You give so much in all that you do, so you need to make sure you're being compensated and treated accordingly. Overall, whatever you choose to do, you need a professional life that offers you room for learning and for showing off what you know. Having a work environment built on teamwork and camaraderie is also a must, as you need people with whom you can share and discuss ideas, as well as people who are willing to share your tough workload.

DAILY AFFIRMATIONS TO HELP YOU GET AHEAD

Through the use of a few daily affirmations, you can attract the career or job advancements that you want. Affirmations are also a great way to open yourself up to opportunities, encouraging positivity even when your career goals aren't panning out as you had hoped.

As an earth sign, you have no qualms about putting in the hours and the discipline to materialize your ideas and desires into something tangible and long-standing like wealth. But as an earth sign ruled by changeable and curious Mercury, you need a career that will pay you well *and* keep you on your toes. By that same token, you also need a career where you can put your brain power to the test and change lives for the better. The following affirmations focus on drawing in the opportunities that you want while also reminding you of just how much you are worth:

- The right job for me provides me with fresh experiences and the chance to learn something new.
- My employer values me and my input; I feel like an important member of the team.
- My coworkers are always ready and willing to lend a helping hand; we are a true team.
- My office environment is busy, productive, and keeps me on my toes in a positive, challenging, and rewarding way.
- I am consistently recognized and celebrated for my genius.
- I make a positive impact on the world around me through my ideas, skills, and desire to be the best at what I do.
- I respect my worth, and I am paid fairly for my work.
- I know that whatever I put my brain power toward I can turn into a reality.
- I have a healthy work-life balance; I have a schedule that works for me.
- I recognize when I need help or assistance, and I am comfortable asking for it.

JOURNAL PROMPTS

Another great resource on your path to success is the use of prompting questions. These questions are designed to get you thinking on a deeper level about what it is that you want and how you can use your skills and past experiences to reach your goals. You're the kind of sign that tends to think best when you can work out a problem in front of you, whether it's on a chalkboard, a computer screen, or in a notebook. These journal prompts will help you do just that while focusing on the elements of the working world, which are the most important—and difficult—for you as a Virgo.

- Think of a time when you felt that you failed. What was something positive that you learned from that experience?
- Sometimes it's the small steps and victories that mean the most, like sending out a resume or completing your vision board. Name at least three small things you've done that you can celebrate right now.
- What's one task that you might be able to delegate to someone else? How can you free up some of your time to do more things you enjoy?

DEALING WITH DISAPPOINTMENT

Okay, so what happens when you've put your all into something and it still doesn't pan out? Disappointments are a part of life, and though it is easy to fall into negative thinking, these setbacks can be overcome and can also be a great learning experience. There are going to be times when you fall short—where your best won't be good enough. It is simply a part of life, and beating yourself up about it is not an option. For one, being hard on yourself doesn't change the past. All it does is make you feel worse about yourself. If you don't get the job you want or something doesn't go as planned—or worse, you lose your job—learn to be gentle with yourself. Instead of worrying too much about the things that went wrong or how much better you wish you could be, give yourself permission to applaud the things that did go right. Learn to celebrate the progress you've made. Yes, even the small wins have value. You sent out a resume? You showed up for an interview? You pitched an idea even though you were a nervous wreck? You gave a project your best effort? All of that has value.

While there is always room for improvement, it can be hard to love yourself where you are, as you are, if you're convinced that the future version of you will always be better. So, cut yourself some slack. Can you perform the act of self-love by accepting who you are in the moment, at any moment? This doesn't mean that you stop pushing yourself toward greatness and growth, it just means that you understand how great you are now. Plus, learning the value of being present to where you are allows you to better roll with the punches. In fact, this goes along with one of your gifts: being a mutable sign. In astrology, each of the four mutable signs—Gemini, Virgo, Sagittarius, and Pisces—represent periods of change and transition. As a Virgo, your job is to make things better through the natural process of change. When taken to the extreme, you can spend too much time worrying about the things both in and out of your control. By pulling back a bit and honoring your current place, you learn what really matters—and what matters is you.

YOUR APPROACH TO WELLNESS

Usually the one with an over-packed or erratic schedule and always willing to lend a helping hand, you have to be careful of taking on too much and spreading yourself too thin. While you thrive on a fast-paced (and at times frenetic) timetable, you have to be diligent about scheduling enough downtime to relax. However, this doesn't mean sleeping your day away, though you will certainly benefit from ample rest. You can still decompress with activities that allow you to have fun and blow off extra steam. Fun and recreation might not be something that always comes easy to you, but with you working as hard as you do, you have to make sure that you play just as hard too. Providing yourself with enough fun and creative outlets to burn off extra energy can help to make sure that that energy doesn't turn into anxiety or nervousness.

MAKING YOUR HOME YOUR CASTLE

Before you grab that tennis racket or hop on that bike, though, you're going to need to make sure your home space is one that you will look forward to coming back to at the end of the day. As a hardworking earth sign, you need a living space that affords you an escape from the daily grind. Here are a few things that will turn your home or living space into your very own getaway:

- Photography or artwork from your travels or favorite places around the world that speak to your inner wanderer.
- A designated room or area of the house that gives you a sense of freedom away from the people you live with or some freedom from the demands of the world.
- Shades of blue or light purple in your work space or common areas to foster fresh ideas and communication.
- White and other neutral shades in the bedroom to help quiet your mind for a more restful sleep.
- A touch of whimsical décor, like a funky lamp, or playful accents, like colorful patterned rugs, to keep the energy light and your spirits high.
- Big windows to give you a sense of freedom. If you don't have big windows, you can use decorative tricks like curtain rods larger than your window or extending your curtains over the wall to make the windows look bigger.
- A well-stocked wine rack or other amenities to entertain and indulge your inner party host.

STAYING GROUNDED: TIPS TO KEEP YOUR FOOTING

Though your home base is covered, you may still find yourself stuck in a place of negative thoughts or unfortunate setbacks. Don't lose heart; even the most prepared Virgo experiences this once in a while. Fortunately, there are easy ways to get back to your productive self.

You've had one of those moments—you may even be in one now: the kind of moment where no matter how hard you try, nothing is coming together the way you want it to, and you feel like you're spinning your wheels. If this happens to you (or is happening now), don't panic. The following exercises will have you back on track and back in your element in no time.

Get Back Into Your Body

As someone who lives in your head, you have a hard time getting out of it once worry or stress takes hold. When this happens, it cuts you off from feeling grounded and connected to your body. One way to combat this is by being aware of your breath. Any time you feel yourself caught up in a rushed, scattered moment, bring your attention to your breath: slow it down and inhale deeply, bringing the breath down into your belly. As you inhale, imagine filling your body with a white, soothing light. Exhale slowly through your mouth. Repeat until you feel calm and centered.

Do Something Self-Affirming

Humility, while noble and relatable, can only get you so far. Before you know it, you get so used to not taking up space that you can all but disappear. This is why it's necessary for you to do things that remind you of your value and beauty. Whether that means creating your own affirmations and mantras that you repeat to yourself daily, adorning yourself with an attention-grabbing statement piece, or taking your creative ideas seriously, affirm your place in the world.

Take a Trip

Though you're an earth sign that thrives on structure and routine, you still have a need to move about and explore new things, or else you run the risk of getting cranky, anxious, or bored. A well-planned, budget-friendly, and well-researched trip helps to feed your dual, mercurial nature (the two halves of you that require freedom of movement as well as consistency). With the right trip to the right destination, you'll get the space you need to clear your mind and spark some fresh ideas.

Watch What You Eat

In astrology, Virgo is connected to the intestines, and like Virgo, the intestines help people to process what their bodies need and eliminate what they don't. This is one reason why you may have issues with food allergies and the like; you are prone to having a sensitive digestive tract. While you may already be a smart eater, sometimes shifting your diet based on your mood can help you stay centered and upbeat. Go for mood-boosting and hydrating (earth needs water!) foods and liquids like watermelon, coconut water, leafy greens, or yogurt to help you to stay present and energized.

Give Yourself a Challenge

There's a saying that goes, "An idle mind is the devil's workshop." It means that when you're in a place where you feel stuck or bored, it's easy to get sucked into unproductive or self-sabotaging thoughts, like constantly clocking how many pounds you've put on or mentally replaying a conversation with your ex. When you channel that energy into something productive and challenging instead, it helps you to feel like you have a sense of purpose. The next time you feel stuck, don't be afraid to break out your vision board (or create one) and get started on your next plan for world domination. Give that brain of yours a workout.

TENDING THE EARTH: TIPS FOR RELIEVING STRESS

If stress still has you feeling like you're spinning out of control, take a deep breath. There are a few great ways to snuff out the stress. You will soon be feeling as relaxed as a tourist lounging on the beach with a refreshing margarita in hand.

As a Virgo, it can be easy for you to get wound up when you have so many things to do and not enough time or hands to do it all. Meanwhile, with your mind always busy making mental to-do lists and worrying over events past, present, and future, you never get to experience true downtime. The following exercises will help you to avoid or alleviate stress so you can finally relax.

Ask for Help

While this may seem like an impossible feat for the zodiac sign that's used to running the show and handling other people's problems, it takes a certain strength of character to admit when you need help. Virgo, you have that strength—use it. Allow others to help you shoulder the load for a change, instead of stressing about it on your own and being stressed and angry about it later.

No Cell Phones, Please

How many times have you fallen asleep with your phone or your laptop in your bed? Thanks to the advancements of technology, there's very little you need to leave your bed for—you can order food and clothing and even set up dates right from the comfort of your pillows. But here's the thing about these gadgets: since they're almost always *on*, you are too, leaving you little room for a restful night's sleep. Leaving them outside of your bedroom, or at least keeping them far away from your bed, helps to create a more peaceful, sleep-friendly environment, allowing you to put your mind and body at rest.

Stick to the Present

In modern healing circles, it is called practicing mindfulness. It's the act of bringing your focus to the present moment instead of allowing your mind to run rampant with worry, laundry lists, regrets, and more. Anytime you feel your brain about to get on that hamster wheel of endless thoughts, try bringing your attention to the current moment. Just focusing on a color, a piece of scenery, a scent in the air, or a pleasurable feeling is enough to bring your mind to a halt.

Do Nothing

This might require a little mindfulness to pull off, but challenge yourself to do nothing. Expel your negative connotations of doing nothing as being "lazy," "unproductive," or "bumming around." Recognize that not every gap of air or time needs to be filled with the act of doing or saying something. If the idea of doing nothing fills you with trepidation, start out with just ten minutes of doing nothing, then work your way up until you can enjoy a chilled-out afternoon without getting ants in your pants.

CHAPTER 7
LIBRA: SEPTEMBER 23–OCTOBER 22

Born with a natural charm that the rest of us can only hope to emulate, you know how to work a crowd or a room effortlessly, making people you've just met feel like old friends by the end of a conversation. While you're also the zodiac's peacekeeper, you're still a force to be reckoned with, especially when it comes to standing up on behalf of others or fighting for justice. For you, romance is a lifestyle, just as fairness and objectivity are. Still, despite your quest for balance, you can easily throw yourself off-kilter by extending yourself too far for the sake of keeping the peace or making others happy.

This chapter is dedicated to giving you the tools to help you to recalibrate and find your center. You'll find guides to navigating relationships with family, friends, and romantic partners. You'll also discover the tricks to staying cool, calm, and collected when stress hits, as well as exercises for creating the career you want.

VENUS RISING

Gwen Stefani, Bruno Mars, Amara La Negra. These are just a handful of the many Libras who have made their mark on the world through their signature style and forays into Venus-related industries such as music, beauty, and fashion.

Paired with your aesthetic planetary ruler, Venus, your natural element is air, which is connected to building social capital and bridges between people, creating a pleasant atmosphere, and inspiring artistic expression. As someone inherently dedicated to fairness and justice, you strive to keep the peace between yourself and those around you, which is why you are known for diplomacy and sharp negotiating skills. Thanks to your keen eye for all things pretty and your love for tranquility, you always know what to say, wear, or do to elevate a room, experience, or relationship. But just because you're an air sign doesn't mean you're an airhead. In fact, fellow Libra Dr. Neil deGrasse Tyson is a prime example of what happens when you pair your sharp mind and penchant for unpacking ideas with a camera-ready personality.

As adept as you are in creating and holding space for others, a big part of your growth and fulfillment centers around learning how to establish relationships with others that are reciprocal and balanced. This learning process may also mean practicing the ability to stick to your guns, and to be a bit more self-preserving by setting healthy boundaries.

Oftentimes, people misinterpret you as disingenuous because of your ability to understand and validate both sides of an argument and your extremely affable personality. What people don't understand is that this behavior is actually a result of fear: the fear of ruffling feathers by "picking sides" in a way that may alienate others or yourself. To avoid allowing your fear to portray you in this light to others, you must learn how to hold space for yourself, recognizing that your identity is not defined by your relationship to others but rather your relationship to yourself. Being able to recognize that there are other people in the room is a gift, but what happens when the room fills up and you get lost in the crowd? In other words, what do you do when you've lost sight of your true self by playing yourself small or by trying to be everything to everyone? There are times when you're going to have to focus less on others and more on yourself. Getting back to who you are will allow you to bring all your wonderful and unique gifts to every aspect of your life, including love.

YOUR APPROACH TO LOVE

A true romantic at heart and the zodiac sign associated with partnership and marriage, you are looking for someone you consider to be your other half— the butter to your bread. Represented by the scales in astrology, you want a partner who understands what it means to be in a collaborative union. Even though you're known to be the unabashed flirt of the zodiac, leaving a swath of admirers in your wake, the person who can successfully woo you is someone who not only has a killer fashion game but also brings something to the table that makes you feel like you are two halves coming together as one. You'll first need a few special tools to keep your flirt game strong.

WOWING WITH COLOR

Even though you could probably teach a crash course in charm and seduction, even the goddess of love herself (Venus) knew how to use everything she had at her disposal to capture the attention of her admirers. You don't need to go out of your way to stop a love interest in their tracks, but it doesn't hurt to have some extra mojo going for you. Using the power of color will keep all eyes on you. The following colors are tailored to complement your Libra charm, wit, and sophistication.

Pink

Associated with romantic and unconditional love, pink is *your* color. If you've lost that loving feeling, or you want to set the mood, wearing a pop of pink will help you to feel youthful, flirty, and oh-so-hip.

Pastels

These shades are similar to neutrals, like cream, because they also provide a stylish and sophisticated look. Depending on the shade, like a pastel yellow or peach, they can also provide a fresh, soft vibe.

Light Blue

Associated with the element of air, light blue shades are your go-to when you're aspiring to a peaceful, laid-back vibe. Blue also evokes clarity of mind and ease in communication, which speaks to your wit and social charm.

SCENTS FOR POWER AND SEDUCTION

Feeling comfortable in your own skin has never been sexier. And power colors aren't the only way to feel sexy in your skin; you can also do so with a few signature fragrances.

Being ruled by a love goddess isn't always easy, especially during those times when you may not be exactly in a loving kind of mood or are too busy (or too tired) for romance. Fortunately, there are fragrances that can help you rebalance the scales and reclaim your sexy, charismatic power. Use these scents to find peace and own your Libran gifts:

Floral

In astrology, flowers are associated with Venusian beauty. It only makes sense then that perfumes and essential oils that contain floral notes are perfectly befitting for a Libra like you. Here are a few floral scents to evoke romance and peace, highlight your beauty, and boost your mood:

- Cherry Blossom
- Gardenia
- Hyacinth
- Lily
- Pansy

Fruity

Juicy and delicious, these fruity notes will have you feeling like the temptress you are, keeping your admirers begging for a taste—point-blank:

- Apple
- Cherry
- Currant
- Peach
- Strawberry

Sweet

Sweet and vivacious like your personality, these notes light up a room just like you do. When you're in a fun and flirty mood, go for fragrances or essential oils that contain these scents:

- Cotton Candy
- Maraschino Cherry
- Marshmallow
- Sorbet

DAILY AFFIRMATIONS FOR LOVE

Now that you've amplified your magnetism, it's important to make sure that you are attracting someone worth your time. Daily affirmations help you to attract the partner that you want by serving as a reminder of what you are and are not looking for in a significant other.

Being the charming beauty that you are, you rarely have trouble finding partners. However, you can be a sucker for a pretty face as well as that addictive falling-in-love feeling, tempting you to choose the "shiny new toy" as opposed to someone with a bit more substance. Coupled with a fear that Libras often have of being alone, this can turn you into a serial dater, moving through relationship after relationship with not-quite-right matches. Although you're the zodiac sign linked to partnership and marriage, you secretly fear that you may never find the right one, and reinforce that fear with relationship choices that don't serve you well.

So how do you know when you've found the right person? When it feels like a true and balanced partnership, without those nagging feelings of something being missing. The following affirmations are designed to help you find the right match for you—a match that is based on mutual respect, attraction, and adoration:

- I am loved and I am complete with or without a partner.
- The right relationship for me is mutually beneficial.
- I am confident in being who I am, just as I am, with the right person for me.
- The right match for me has looks, charm, wit, and a big heart.
- The perfect relationship for me is full of both substance and romance.
- When I communicate with my partner, I feel heard and respected.
- My partner surprises me with gifts and tokens of affection.
- The sexual chemistry with my perfect match keeps me happy and on my toes.

DEALING WITH HEARTBREAK AND BREAKUPS

Affirmations in hand, you may still come up against an inevitable heartbreak or two in your life. Although breakups are something that you dread—and understandably so (who actually likes a breakup?)—there are a few ways you can overcome heartbreak without it overcoming *you*.

Because you're an air sign, you are able to remain rational and objective enough to get over heartbreak quickly, especially since there's usually no shortage of admirers waiting in the wings. Be that as it may, breakups can be devastating. This is largely due to how much you're willing to invest in a partnership, even at the risk of losing yourself in the process. When you've spent a lot of time and energy focusing on your partner and your relationship, it can be hard to regain your sense of personal identity. Reclaiming this identity is the key to getting over heartbreak. There's a saying that goes, "Who were you before the world told you who you should be?" This is a powerful and thought-provoking question to ask yourself in the face of a breakup. Who are you outside of a relationship? How would you define yourself? What kinds of things turn you on? Specifically, what excites you and makes you feel alive? If you struggle with the answers, you can instead use this period of being single to start off with a blank slate. What kind of ideas and dreams do you have that are waiting for you to act on them? What kind of experiences are you craving to have that can be uniquely your own?

However, don't let a breakup be the catalyst for putting yourself first. Start making yourself a priority now. One way you can do this is by honoring your authentic self. Changing for a partner doesn't work. Growing with a partner while respecting each other's individuality is what helps to keep a relationship alive. Another way that you can begin putting yourself first is by making solo dates a thing. You'd be surprised at how many people are afraid that going out alone will be seen by others as weird. Taking yourself out is both a fun and empowering thing to do. By keeping your own company, you're practicing an act of self-affirmation. You're saying "I love me." Plus, when you "date" yourself, you're showing love interests that you lead a full life with your own interests and activities—and that is quite the turn-on. Think about it, if you can't stand to be alone with yourself, why would anyone else? Let a partner be a complement to you and your life, not something to complete it. This goes double for your relationships with friends and family.

HANDLING RELATIONSHIPS WITH FAMILY AND FRIENDS

Family relationships, especially with your parents, are often tricky for you, because no matter how independent or successful you become, it may always feel like you're still living under their thumb. You may feel like you have to consistently justify how you live your life and make decisions, or you may find yourself constantly seeking out their approval. As a Libra, you aim to please and live in harmony with others, especially when it comes to your loved ones. However, many of your lessons, especially within family dynamics, will involve learning to be happy with yourself and your life, regardless of who's watching or who approves. Fending off questions about your love life or your career choices might be something that you've learned how to avoid or give the "right" answers to even if they're not necessarily true. However, you must get comfortable with standing up for yourself in the face of a well-meaning yet overbearing parent or family member. You know what is best for you, and sometimes family traditions need to be left in the past—just because something is the norm doesn't mean that it's the only correct way or still applies to you today. Keep this in mind the next time your family starts peppering you with "Why aren't you married yet?"

As for your friendships, there's a saying that goes, "Show me your friends and I'll show you who you are." Basically, you can tell a lot about a person by their circle of friends. As a social butterfly, you gravitate toward people who can elevate your social standing in some way, which usually means that the names of powerful and influential people populate your cell phone's contact list. While rubbing shoulders with the movers and shakers is not a bad thing, needing to be among the in-crowd makes you prone to defining your identity based solely on your proximity to these people. Instead, you should base your friendships on a person's genuineness. Establishing friendships with genuine people who care about and respect you allows you to be your true self sans fear.

YOUR APPROACH TO CAREER

Being true to yourself and your needs isn't only for love and relationships, it applies to your career aspirations too. As the sign ruled by Venus (the planet of pleasure, art, and beauty), it's no surprise that you are drawn to creative fields like the visual and performing arts, fashion, and design. With your pulse on the trends, usually light-years before they happen, you have a knack for hitting your audience in just the right spot, creating an emotional and inspiring connection to your work. Since Libra also represents fairness and justice, you may also find yourself within the legal system as a judge, lawyer, or other law official.

Not only do you need a job that provides you with a creative outlet, but you also need a job that provides you with a sense of fulfillment in helping others and making the world a happier place. This is why jobs that make you feel like just another cog in the wheel won't appeal to you. Jobs that lack heart or emotional fulfillment won't cut it for you either—while others may be able to work long and hard for a paycheck alone, you're not someone who can sell your soul for a dollar, regardless of how ambitious you are. With the goddess of love as your patron saint, saying that you need to love what you do is no exaggeration.

DAILY AFFIRMATIONS TO HELP YOU GET AHEAD

Using affirmations is a great way to attract the exciting, fulfilling career or job advancements that you want. Affirmations are also a great way to open yourself up to opportunities, encouraging positivity even when your career goals aren't panning out as you had hoped.

Being a child of Venus, you have the gift of attraction—the ability to draw in the people and the things you want based on your charm and beauty. Sometimes this can be easy for you to forget in a world that values Mars's methods (competition, aggressive action, etc.) for getting the job done. Use the following affirmations as both a reminder of your gifts and as a way to supercharge your plans for success. As the old saying goes, "If you can believe it, you can achieve it."

- I bring beauty and healing to the world through my art and creative talent.
- Great companies want to hire me because I deeply believe in what I do.
- I have my finger on the pulse and know what people want. I trust my instincts and deliver results.
- People want to pay me well for my work; I am a magnet for money.
- I have a positive, professional relationship with my coworkers.
- I know I am worthy of office relationships that make me feel valued and good about myself.
- I have a healthy balance between my personal life and my professional life.
- I recognize when it's time to leave a job and take the steps necessary to find a new one.
- I trust my gut when it comes to my professional decisions; I lead with my intuition.
- I know when I am in the right job, because it makes me feel like I am making an actual difference in the lives of others.

JOURNAL PROMPTS

Another way to put yourself on the path to success is through the use of prompting questions. These questions push you to dig deeper into what it is you are looking for and how you can use past experiences to attain it.

When making changes or improvements to an area of your life, it helps to be able to bring your thoughts and ideas out of your head, getting them off the mental hamster wheel where they just go around and around. By putting your thoughts down on paper, you can identify fears that may be holding you back, as well as the resources that you already have in hand to help you to get where you want to go. These journal prompts are designed to remind you of your resources and help you remember that you've got what it takes to solve your own problems:

- Think of a time when you had to step up and take the lead. List at least three positive things you learned about yourself from that situation. How can you apply those qualities toward meeting your next big goal?
- Come up with at least five things that make you stand out from your peers. How can you put these gifts to use on a regular basis?
- What are at least two steps you can take right now to get you closer to a more fulfilling place in your career?

DEALING WITH DISAPPOINTMENT

Even when you have all the right stuff, setbacks are a part of the working world. Big or small, there will most likely be disappointments along the way to success. Luckily, there are a few ways to handle these situations without losing your confidence.

As someone who prides yourself on what you've accomplished, you don't take the idea of losing lightly. Your attitude toward success is one of the things that makes you so ambitious and unrelenting when it comes to getting what you want, using your wit, charm, and ambition to do so. You also have an innate understanding of the kind of power that a stellar reputation and money can bring you.

Although being ambitious is not a bad thing, nor is material success, the trouble arises when you place too much emphasis on these things. This doesn't mean that you should scale back on pursuing your goals or that you should play yourself small, but you may need to shift your perspective on what it means to win and to be successful. Otherwise, if you attach your worth to what you have and don't have, you will see a disappointment— such as not getting the promotion or the job you want—as a reflection of you as a person. It's not. Sometimes not getting what you want doesn't have anything to do with you. Maybe the promotion was already promised to someone else. Maybe the person interviewing you is a terrible inter- viewer, asking questions that not only throw you off, but throw the inter- view off too. It happens.

Know that if you do suffer a disappointment or find yourself feeling bad about not being where you want to be professionally, it's okay to acknowledge your feelings—just don't allow this moment to knock the air out of you. Instead, use this moment to make peace with yourself and to toss out any outworn beliefs that you may have about success. Aside from money and clout, what are some things that make you successful? What is it about you that makes you the bee's knees? Don't limit yourself to just one expression of success: flourish on your own terms. This positive twist on an unfortunate situation will lead to more positivity in other aspects of your life as well, including your personal well-being.

YOUR APPROACH TO WELLNESS

As an air sign, you like to live life on the go and tend to do best in settings where you can socialize and have fun. However, there are ways that you can overindulge on fun, whether it's frequently keeping late hours at the many events you attend or indulging in fast food and sugary treats. It is important to make sure your living space provides you with the opportunity to slow down once in a while and maintain your well-being.

MAKING YOUR HOME YOUR CASTLE

As an air sign, you live a whirlwind lifestyle, so you need a place that will allow you to rebalance and recharge so you can continue to take the world by storm. Here are a few things that appeal to both your aesthetic and functional sides:

- Dark colors, like burgundy or navy blue, combined with neutrals, like ivory or taupe, to create a sense of grounding, calm, and stability.
- A designated work or office space that can help you to stay focused and organized and finish what you start.
- Low-maintenance houseplants that accommodate your on-the-go lifestyle while representing a flow of wealth and abundance.
- Furniture and other decorative items with sharp, crisp lines that provide you with a sense of organization and structure. Industrial designs also work well.
- Well-researched, high-quality items that not only elevate the aesthetic of your living space, but also appreciate over time, helping to elevate your financial security too.
- Keep clocks out of your bedroom for a more restful sleep. If you need an alarm to wake you, try putting it in an area that's outside of your bedroom but close enough for you to hear it. If you use your cell phone as your alarm clock, keep it as far away from your bed as possible.
- Free weights to help decompress and ground your body and relieve stress.

GETTING FRESH AIR: TIPS FOR HELPING YOU FEEL RENEWED

Although you're a mover and a shaker, your busy lifestyle doesn't prevent you from being prone to burnout and illness. As a matter of fact, you can be quite sensitive to stress and overstimulation, which often manifests as chronic fatigue, anxiety, or a weakened immune system. Also, while you are a people person, keeping company with too many of the wrong people can drain you just as much as any sensitive water sign. The good news is that, along with medical care, there are some preventative measures that you can take to keep yourself balanced and feeling good.

Feeling like you would much rather wear sweats and a T-shirt than one of your more stylish ensembles? Or like you aren't as sociable or creatively inspired as you usually are? It looks like you've hit a wall and could use a reset. The following exercises will help you get your glow back to divine levels.

Embrace Your Weird

As an image-conscious sign, you can all-too-easily fall into the trap of worrying about what others think of you or attempting to keep up with the in-crowd. This will leave you feeling creatively and energetically blocked. The next time you find yourself stressing over how others see you, embrace your weird. Make a game of it: have a thing for playing ukulele rock music or writing about time-jumping space pigeons? Good. Sink into your uniqueness, especially when it comes to those things that people may have attempted to put you down for or tease you about. Take joy in the things that you do differently, as this is where your creative energy comes from.

Take a Day Trip

Since Libra is linked to the element of air, it's no shocker that you need to move around and circulate, much like air does. Air is also defined by its intellectual characteristics, as the mission of air signs is to gather and share information. This is where travel comes in. It doesn't need to be anything pricey or lengthy—you can pick a part of the city you've never been to or a place a few towns away. The point is to not only welcome in some fresh energy, but also to be inspired by something new. Bonus points if it involves a cultural festival, museum, or library.

Go Where Your Heart Leads You

For those times when you need a dose of inspiration or feel like you've lost your way, dive down into your heart space. What does it want? It doesn't necessarily have to be anything extravagant, it just needs to be something that you feel drawn toward. Maybe this means signing up for that improv class that you've been wanting to take. Or maybe it means waking up on a weekday and deciding that you'd rather spend the day at a museum you've been wanting to visit. Whatever you decide to do, let it be something that turns you on just thinking about it.

Call On Your Friends

As the sign related to teamwork and partnership, you usually have no qualms with pitching in to help out others—but who's on Team Libra? It's important that you have some people in your life with whom you can be tender and vulnerable. If you already have friends like this in your corner, congratulations! Now get on the horn and reach out to them.

Role-Play

Sometimes there's nothing better to help you feel like yourself than pretending to be someone else. You're feeling a little edgy today? Throw on your leather jacket and let your "dangerous" side out to play. Feeling more along the lines of Hollywood glam? Let your inner movie star shine. Whatever your mood, celebrating the different facets of who you are will boost your confidence and creativity.

KEEPING IT EASY-BREEZY: TIPS FOR RELIEVING STRESS

Now that you've got your glow back, there are a few things to keep in mind to make sure that it sticks around when things get a little overwhelming. As a sign that tends to give so much of yourself to others in both your professional and private life, you can succumb to the pressure that others put on you through their demands, leading to stress, nervous tension, and burnout. In this section, you'll find tips for alleviating—and even avoiding—this pressure.

Practice the Art of Receiving

How many times has someone offered to do something for you, and you've met their offer with a "No thanks, I've got it," or, "It's okay, you don't have to"? How many times has someone offered you a compliment and you tried to downplay it or shrug it off? If the answer is too many times to count, you're blocking your blessings. The archetype of Venus in astrology is associated with reciprocity and receptivity. If something is going out, like love or money, something should be coming in, like a favor from a family member or a friend picking up the tab for lunch. This will keep the harmony flowing.

When you're out of balance, it can often translate into an inability to be open to receiving, as well as an inability to recognize what you already have. Many Libras are prone to pouring themselves out—sacrificing themselves for others and putting their desires or needs last. What is left over in these situations is an empty vessel. The next time someone compliments you or offers to do something for you, don't second guess or refuse it. Receive it with your heart open wide.

Make Time for You and Only You

Be more protective of how you spend your time. This means being more careful about the things you agree to do for others. You don't need to cut everyone off or treat people coldly, but by being protective of your time, you're creating a boundary for others and also putting your needs first. Spending time on your own also gets you out of the habit of needing other people around to keep you busy or to entertain you. Remember: don't let the fear of being alone deter you from finding happiness in your own company.

Don't Sweat the Small Stuff

Sometimes, when you're too close to a subject or find yourself hung up on the details, you lose sight of what really matters. When you find yourself getting overwhelmed or distressed over a tough choice, try to shift your perspective. This may mean drafting a list of pros and cons, talking about how you feel to a trusted friend or therapist, or challenging the old, worn-out stories you've been telling yourself (journal writing is a great way to do this).

Make Peace with Your Anger

Whew! This may be a tough one to do, especially when you try so hard to be likeable. Yet, here's the thing about honoring your anger: it helps you to speak your truth and maintain necessary boundaries that are vital to your well-being. So, the next time you feel yourself hitting your boiling point, don't swallow it. Don't try to sugarcoat it or rationalize your way through—relish it. Let it roll around on your tongue. Let it spill onto paper or into the street. Practice saying *no* and leaving it at that. Also practice telling someone just how you feel. You are not here to be anyone's doormat.

CHAPTER 8
SCORPIO: OCTOBER 23–NOVEMBER 21

Radiating a smoldering, pulsating energy that pulls in friends and crushes alike like moths to a flame, you are a magnetic person who very few can resist. Adopting an all-or-nothing approach to the world, you don't take life, nor your connections with others, lightly. There's very little in life that you haven't seen, from the highs to the very low lows, bestowing on you the courage and deep insight to take on just about anything. You teach the rest of us how to get the most out of what life has to offer through the deep emotional experiences that fuel your core. Trouble arises when you're feeling threatened or off your game, which can lead to a string of unhealthy relationships with others—and yourself.

The information that follows in this chapter is dedicated to helping you maintain your edge with as few rough patches as possible. You'll explore ways to feel better in your body and reduce stress, improve relationships with your friends and family, and of course, keep your admirers wanting you.

THE LOVER AND THE FIGHTER

You are often the most misunderstood sign in astrology. This is because of the themes that Scorpio is associated with: death, rebirth, and transformation—all of which are avoided in society, as they are considered either too heavy, uncomfortable, or inappropriate to tackle head-on. Not for you, though. You're always ready to dive into them headfirst, taking whoever is brave enough to go along for the ride with you. Not one to skim the surface, you thrive on emotional depth and exploring the subconscious and its themes. Not only do you have the keen insight into human behavior that gives you the ability to spot people and their motivations a mile away, but you also have a mystery and magnetism about you that both pushes people away and attracts them to you. People can easily misunderstand you if they're not paying close enough attention, especially if they link your fearless exploration of taboo topics as being all about sex. The truth is that you are looking for a sense of wholeness within yourself and with a partner by way of absolute intimacy and unfiltered emotional honesty. At your core, you desire to exist beyond borders and limitations—to live in a place where souls touch, a place where soul-deep healing can take place and personal power can be reclaimed in the face of frightening, character-testing experiences. Co-ruled by passionate Mars and fearless Pluto, you are turned on by the messy, mysterious sides of the human experience.

For all your strength, you are also incredibly sensitive. This sensitivity is one of the gifts that makes you a deeply devoted and loving partner and friend. However, when that sensitivity is triggered by your insecurities, you struggle with holding grudges. Being co-ruled by the two planets related to anger, power, and traumatic experiences, you don't take your feelings lightly. Overall, your lesson is to learn how to love yourself with the same ferocity that you would a soul mate. By loving yourself that fiercely and that deeply, you acknowledge that: 1. what's meant for you will always find you, and 2. when you find the courage to let go of what doesn't serve you, you make room for the things you want to enter your life—soul mate included.

YOUR APPROACH TO LOVE

Forever is the word that describes your approach to love, as when you fall in love, you never let go. As the zodiac sign linked to power and intimacy, you are both afraid of and turned on by this fact. You do want to experience the depths of emotion, but you struggle to let go of your power. If you're going to be willing to bare your soul to a partner, they better be worth the trouble. You don't mind testing them to prove their worthiness either. Some might say that you play games with your partners' heads and hearts, when in reality you're just trying to dig deep enough to see if they can handle the likes of you. The person who captures your heart and wins your undying love is someone who won't be easily rattled by the weightier issues in life or the skeletons in your closet.

WOWING WITH COLOR

Speaking of capturing hearts, there are a few ways to turn your confidence and your powers of seduction up to full blast. As the zodiac sign associated with mystery, secrets, and intrigue, you tend to play your cards close to your chest to maintain the elements of power and control. This means that when it comes to that initial meeting with a love interest, the less you have to say or reveal about yourself, the better. Utilize your power colors as part of your recipe for romance and seduction to keep your edge of mystery.

Black

The color that is absent of color, black represents death, mystery, and all the things that we would rather keep hidden. In other words, it's perfect for a Scorpio like you. Also considered to be a color of power, black is your go-to when you want to exude the confidence and dangerous allure of a sexy, no-nonsense secret agent. Bonus: black is also known for warding off negative energy, which is a must for a malleable water sign like you.

Crimson

Deep, bloodlike reds such as crimson not only complement your passionate and insatiable nature, but they also represent sophistication and balls-to-the-wall determination. Go for these shades when you want to dress to kill.

Deep Purple

The darker the shade of purple, the more beguiling it is. Go for deep purple hues when you want a temporary break from black but still want to honor your inner sorceress. Purple is also associated with the Third Eye, which represents intuition. Being a water sign, your instincts and intuition are your superpowers.

SCENTS FOR POWER AND SEDUCTION

As intuitive as you are, you know how powerful the senses can be when aroused by passion and eroticism. So, with your seductive colors now at play, you can heighten the senses even more through the power of scent.

Raw, magnetic, unstoppable. These are just a few of the words used to describe you—and that's before nine a.m. Use these fragrances, or blend them into your own creation, to release your inner power and skills of seduction.

Spicy

Ruled by the hot and all-consuming Mars, you radiate heat all on your own. But since you're a sign that doesn't do subtlety, use these notes to turn up the heat, and your sense of confidence, even more:

- Clove
- Pepper

- Sumac
- Wasabi

Musky

Also known as animalistic notes, these musky elements make up the scents that are reminiscent of natural pheromones, which is great for stimulating that post-sex vibe. If *F*ck, Marry, Kill* is your mood of the day (okay, it's your mood *every* day), go for essential oils or perfumes that contain these notes to employ the art of seduction:

- Amber
- Musk

- Patchouli
- Tuber

Resins

Used across centuries for both witchcraft and religious rituals, resins are intense, long-lasting, and provide a spiritual experience. Use these scents for their healing properties and their ability to uplift your soul:

- Benzoin
- Dragon's Blood
- Frankincense

DAILY AFFIRMATIONS FOR LOVE

Using affirmations is another great way to attract the love that you want. Affirmations remind you of what is important to you in a relationship while also encouraging positivity in the face of a letdown.

Trust is not something you take lightly, which means that while you long to have a ride-or-die partner by your side, you are also deathly afraid of being betrayed, manipulated, or abandoned by the one you love. Out of your fear of being vulnerable, you can make it hard for potential love interests to get inside your heart—especially when past wounds come into play. While your past experiences hold valuable lessons, you instead use them to create self-fulfilling prophecies about love interests, ending a relationship before it's had the chance to begin. The following affirmations are designed to help you release your fears around love while also helping you to tap into your potent powers of attraction, drawing in the kind of relationship you truly want:

- I am capable of having a healthy and emotionally fulfilling relationship.
- I am willing and brave enough to open my heart to love.
- I release my past partners and relationships, and I receive the lessons they taught me about how I deserve to be loved.
- The perfect partner for me is trustworthy, loyal, and dedicated to me and the happiness of our relationship.
- The right partner for me is stable, secure, and always there when I need someone to lean on.
- My partner is someone who I can talk to about anything and everything, no matter how deep or intense.
- The perfect relationship for me is full of passion, intimacy, and toe-curling sex.
- When I am with my partner, I feel loved, healed, and confident that I am with the person who was made for me.

DEALING WITH HEARTBREAK AND BREAKUPS

Sometimes, despite the planning and hard work, breakups still occur. Heartbreak is a natural course of life and love. Fortunately, there are a few easy ways to navigate these emotional waters while staying afloat.

Getting over a heartbreak is never easy, but as the zodiac sign that feels everything to the nth degree, it can take you months or even years to get over a relationship gone sour. Your unwavering, no-matter-the-circumstances love can at times seem like both a gift and a curse. Your die-hard loyalty and devotion is what tends to draw in your admirers in droves, each one hoping to be the one to break through the barbed wire that surrounds your heart. Because of your need for security, you find yourself trying to force a stale or unhealthy relationship to keep going, even at the sake of your own happiness. Likewise, because of your need for emotional depth within an intimate relationship, you can mistake destructive power struggles and emotional, roller-coaster relationships as the kind of intimacy you crave. In reality, the only thing these relationships are doing is further triggering your fears around love. In the end, getting over a breakup requires that you let go—of your ex, and of any resentments or anger that you may have toward them. So, start cutting those cords, Scorpio.

But where do you start? One word: forgiveness. You're rolling your eyes now, but understand that forgiveness doesn't mean letting a person off the hook or denying your pain. It just means that you are letting go of the resentment, anger, and old memories to keep yourself from becoming consumed by them. In essence, choosing to forgive someone means that you are choosing yourself. The act of forgiving someone takes a lot of strength, because it involves admitting to the role that you played in the relationship, instead of pointing fingers and laying blame. Once you can start to see the story from both angles, it becomes easier to bid a person adieu. You can move toward forgiveness by writing a letter (that you'll never send) to your ex, wishing them well on their journey, imagining yourself cutting the cord between you, or simply saying "I release you." Make sure to forgive yourself in the process. Learning to forgive yourself and others will also be an important part of your relationships with family members and friends.

HANDLING RELATIONSHIPS WITH FAMILY AND FRIENDS

While you define and pride yourself on your deepest bonds, the relationships that you share with your family tend to be a bit more challenging and complex than you'd like. It's not that you don't love your family, it's just that you need lots of independence to maintain your own sense of well-being and happiness. This may mean leaving a few zip codes between you and your parents or close relatives. It may also mean breaking free of old family norms or dynamics that impede your self-expression. Getting along with your family may also require that you practice acceptance. This doesn't mean letting your folks erode your boundaries: it means accepting them as they are, which can save you a headache of trying to control something you can't. Ultimately, when you try to control others and their behavior (a habit of many a Scorpio), not only do you fail to do so, but you also put yourself in a defensive place where you always have to be right. This can also make loved ones feel as though they are being manipulated.

With regard to your friendships, you often handpick your friends with great care and forethought because, let's face it, not everyone is trustworthy enough to get past your barbed wire. Flaky folks and gossipy friends are not something you have to worry about. Your sharp instincts and keen intuition usually enable you to know who you can trust and who you can't. What you should be cautious about is being your friends' therapist. Water signs—Cancer, Scorpio, and Pisces—have a tendency to find themselves in situations where people, especially strangers, feel comfortable enough to spill their deepest, darkest secrets to them. You possess a knack for understanding the human condition, which tends to make you a natural psychologist. Still, when people are constantly dumping their emotions and situations on you, it becomes quite draining. Some may also take advantage of your listening skills, like the friend that always calls on you when they need an ear, but never checks to see how you're doing. This is when you need to focus on being more discerning about who you make yourself available to, as well as when. This practice of discernment will also benefit you in other areas of your life as well, such as your profession.

YOUR APPROACH TO CAREER

Ruled by planetary powerhouses Mars and Pluto, you are naturally a powerhouse yourself, bringing the same level of intensity to your career that you bring to everything else. This translates to a take-no-prisoners approach to your career goals and ambitions. For you, failure is not an option, and you refuse to let anything or anyone stand in your way on the path to greatness. Not one for making moves without a strategy, your powerful instincts, laser-like focus, and secret-agent approach help you get rid of the competition before they even know what hit them. However, make sure that you don't become so obsessed with winning that you lose your integrity or perspective along the way, which might push you to take a by-any-means-necessary approach to success.

You rarely, if ever, do anything half-heartedly, which means that your career path must be something that you can pursue with everything you've got, providing you the opportunity to push your limits, either physically or mentally. This is why some Scorpios become skilled athletes, while other Scorpios pursue fields where they can put their detective and research skills to use. Your ability to heal others also draws you to fields that deal with psychology and counseling or rehabilitation. Since Scorpio is a sign that also handles other people's resources, financial advising is a common job choice as well.

As you embark on your career path, affirmations can be a great tool in helping you to reach your goals. These motivational phrases not only ensure that you are putting out the positive vibes that will draw opportunities to you, but also remind you of things to recall when taking on a new job, working toward a promotion, or reconsidering your current job.

DAILY AFFIRMATIONS TO HELP YOU GET AHEAD

As one of the zodiac's toughest go-getters, there isn't much that you're willing to let get in your way on the road to success. However, you can quickly get stopped in your tracks when you let others define your greatness. With the help of the following affirmations, you are not only affirming what makes you unique, but also your ability to craft the kind of future that you want, based on your own values:

- I leave my own unique stamp on all that I do; I offer something special that no one else can.
- The perfect job for me is one that fills me with passion and drive.
- I know that my losses are only opportunities for me to get closer to what is really meant for me.
- I know that I am more than my professional achievements or losses; I am a complex being that exists beyond external rewards.
- I attract money and wealth with ease; wherever I go, I can create opportunities for myself.
- I maintain my integrity and character in all that I do; I define and respect my core values.

- I am recognized in my field as a force to be reckoned with; I am respected and admired.
- My work keeps me consistently and happily challenged; I love what I do.
- I am committed to my personal development and growth; I strive to always be my best.
- I am unbothered by negative criticism or lack of praise; I define my success.

JOURNAL PROMPTS

In addition to these affirmations, it will also help you in pursuing your career goals to draw on the experiences that have brought you to where you are now. As a powerhouse of the zodiac, you thrive on intensity, whether it's your work schedule or the work at hand. You have no qualms about putting in sleepless nights to achieve your goals. Although this kind of work ethic is enviable, you have to be cautious of burning out. You also desire recognition and accolades from others for a job well done. This can lead to living solely for the spotlight. Through the following journal exercises, you'll explore how to best address these challenges and what you might be able to learn from them:

- How can you bring more balance to your workday? In what ways can you make more time to chill out?
- Do you think criticism can be helpful? How so? Name a time when someone offered you a critique that turned out to be helpful. What was the result?
- If you didn't receive attention or praise from others for your work, would it still be meaningful to you? Would your work still have value if there was no applause?

DEALING WITH DISAPPOINTMENT

Being skipped over or having your efforts go unnoticed can still feel like a blow to your confidence. Fortunately, there are ways to handle these disappointments without taking them personally. Sometimes life kicks your butt, or a roadblock gets in your way—you get passed over for a promotion, lose your job, or perhaps didn't do as well as you would have liked in that interview. Things happen, and it's important not to take it personally. As a zodiac sign that feels every emotion to the nth degree, you can easily perceive a slight where there may not necessarily be one. It's also important to remember that when you focus too much on external rewards, like a job title or a pat on the back from the boss, you lose sight of what matters. The true reward lies in being who you are, sans the attention, labels, or praise that others may give to you. The key to dealing with disappointment is recognizing that no one person, experience, or thing can determine how successful you are or will be. Instead of stewing in your feelings over a disappointment, consider using your time to map out other options or to develop a backup plan. Another thing that will help you to deal with a disappointment is a release ritual or exercise. Maybe this means ripping up a rejection letter, or writing the situation down on paper and burning it. The idea behind the ritual is to release yourself from the disappointment and let go of something that you cannot change.

Being a fixed water sign, you like to keep things as they are, with very few changes. Although this is a good thing when it comes to building security and stability, it can also cause a lack of growth in your career. As such, it might be a good time to think about how you might switch up your game plan or take a new approach. This might mean making changes or taking risks in your career that may not necessarily make sense to others. Another thing that may be helpful to you is to examine whether a negative job situation or setback is really as bad as it seems. Losing a job, for example, is undoubtedly a discouraging and stressful situation; however, by standing back and taking a look at the situation with a little perspective, you may see that it was necessary to lose that job to make space for a position that's better aligned for you. Maybe this means making a list of pros and cons about the situation and focusing more on the pros. Maybe it means seeking out the wise counsel of a friend or mentor. You crave intimacy, but because it can be hard for you to open up and trust others, you often suffer through things alone. Talking (or venting) to someone close to you about what you're feeling instead of trying to shoulder through it alone may reveal a solution or provide you with some needed words of encouragement and advice.

YOUR APPROACH TO WELLNESS

With your incredible drive and your love of extremes, you have no qualms about pushing yourself or your body to its limits. This means that you can usually be found working long hours or crazy schedules to accommodate your ambition, passion, and intensity. Despite this, you can also push yourself toward a burnout when you don't take frequent breaks to recharge your batteries. That's why this chapter is geared toward helping you recognize when you may need a break and showing you ways that you can ramp up your self-care habits and routines.

Before you dash off on your next mission, though, make sure you have a soft place to land when you're done. This means creating a living space that fits your specific Scorpio needs.

MAKING YOUR HOME YOUR CASTLE

Some might peg you as being possessive or territorial, but you just like your space to be exactly that—your space. You need a bat cave of sorts that is secluded and private enough to be able to recharge your batteries and cook up your next winning strategy. Here are a few items for building your own secret lair:

- Funky, eclectic, and custom-made pieces that give you the feel of a space that's all your own. Bohemian-style accents and items would fall under this umbrella.
- Art tools and materials that you can use on creative projects to release stress and negative emotions.
- Organizational and easy-storage items that can accommodate your busy schedule and help you with locating things at a moment's notice.
- Gadgets that can help you to simplify your life as well as provide a source of entertainment for hours on end, namely for those times when you need a break from the rest of the world. This could be anything from a wireless speaker system to a gaming console.
- A designated space for your gadgets so they don't interfere with your sleep.
- Bright or contrasting colors that stimulate ideas and the feel-good chemicals in your brain.
- Low-maintenance furniture that doesn't require a lot of upkeep or attention. You're too busy to worry about keeping cushions fluffy or what's the best way to get out a wine stain.

GETTING FRESH WATER: TIPS FOR FINDING YOUR FLOW

Being a water sign also means that you pick up on others' moods and feelings, making you susceptible to accumulating lots of negative energy. Guarding yourself against this requires that you take lots of time to yourself to release those energies and get back to feeling like yourself again. Luckily, getting your flow back is as easy as a few simple exercises.

You're a zodiac sign that needs to be mindful of when life has become too rigid or stale. As a Scorpio, this means that you may have to go through periods of rebirth or regeneration in order to find your flow and get things moving again. The following are a few exercises to help you hit the reset button.

Release It to the Water

Much of your energy is spent in the emotional realm. With your super-powered sixth sense, it doesn't take much for you to pick up on what other people are thinking and feeling—without them even saying a word. On top of this, you also have your own emotions that you're constantly churning, analyzing, reliving, and at times, sulking over. This means that you end up accumulating lots of emotional energy over time that can turn into bitterness, depression, anxiety, etc.

Water is one way to release these emotions. Astrologically speaking, the element of water is considered to have a cleansing and healing effect on the mind and body. Even the act of being near a large body of water, like the ocean, can have a healing effect on you. You can take it one step further with a ritual geared toward dropping or releasing your burdens into the water. Try writing down what you want to release (you can even start your sentences with *I release*) on paper—environmentally friendly paper is preferred. Take your paper to an ocean, river, or another body of moving water and drop it in, allowing the water to carry it away from you.

Mix Self-Pleasure with Intention

You know that you can use orgasms as a tool for pleasure and release, but did you know that you can use them to amplify your intentions too? In witchcraft circles this is called *sex magick*, but for a deeply passionate and magnetic sign like you, you might as well call it "getting sh*t done." The next time you feel out of sorts or off your game, don't turn to the usual boring sex—turn things up a notch by channeling your sexual energy into productivity. First, pick a time when you'll be undisturbed. You can also time it with a specific phase of the Moon, like a New Moon, which represents fresh starts and new beginnings. Then prepare your space in a way that makes you feel sexy—you can use candles, sexy music, or wear a special silk robe just for the occasion. You might even consider taking a bath beforehand with a sexy essential oil like rose or patchouli. As you pleasure yourself, think about something you'd like to achieve or manifest. The goal is to hold this thought in your mind the entire time as you bring yourself to orgasm, as this is when your magnetism is the strongest. By the time you're done, you should feel like you're back in charge and ready to conquer anything.

Spend Time Abroad

While most people get a kick out of travel, for you it's a part of your lifeblood. There's something about setting up camp in another country or city that not only makes you feel at home (ah, that air of mystery!), but also gives you the opportunity to cocoon yourself away from the world. It's not uncommon for you to venture off to a distant or secluded locale in search of solitude, creative inspiration, and refreshment.

Practice Discipline

As a sign motivated by desire, you have no trouble giving in to it for the things that you love so much. However, if those things aren't necessarily healthy for you, like sex with the horrible ex that you keep going back to, then it's time to exercise that ironclad willpower of yours. Saying *no* to something (or someone) doesn't mean that you have to suffer by doing without. It just means that you're saying *yes* for something much better to fill that space. Plus, a good detoxing period can help you with clearing your body, mind, and soul to give you the reset you need. With just a few simple strategies, you can make the most of your detox.

RIDING THE WAVE: TIPS FOR RELIEVING STRESS

As a zodiac sign that loves being in control, you know how uncomfortable it feels when life seems to have a mind of its own. The following suggestions are easy ways to find your calm in the center of life's storms.

Make Art Your Therapy

There's a reason why people find art so important: not only does it have the capacity to stimulate and open up minds, but it also has the capacity to heal. Just think about your favorite song or film, and how it makes you feel. Whether your interest is in painting, dance, photography, or music, make art your therapy. You don't need to worry about being artistically inclined. You don't even have to share your art with others. You just need a peaceful space where you can let your imagination run wild.

Blow Off Some Steam

As hotheaded as your fellow Martian Aries, it doesn't take a lot to get you riled up. While you may be able to hide it a bit better than Aries, you still don't like having your buttons pushed. When it comes to stress, frustration can be a trigger. However, instead of holding on to your frustration or plotting revenge, look to ways that you can blow off steam. This could be something like having sex, attending a kickboxing class, or going for a run. Burning off steam doesn't have to be physical either; try cranking up some of your angriest music and screaming at the top of your lungs.

Look for the Good News

Your spot-on intuition and ability to see things as they are makes it hard to pull one over on you. It also makes you susceptible to expecting the bad in everything. The trouble with this is that it can exacerbate any stress or anxiety that you may already be feeling. As a malleable water sign, it's vital that you have "psychic" boundaries in place to keep from absorbing too much negative information. No doubt that it's important to stay aware of current events and to keep an eye out for shady people, but when you make a practice of seeking good news, you are taking care of yourself. Try to find twice as many good stories as you do bad news. If all else fails, you can just watch cute animal videos.

Honor Rejection

There's a saying that goes, "Rejection is protection." Basically, it means that if you get rejected for something, there's a good chance that it wasn't meant for you in the first place. Just think back to all the times you may have tried to force something to go your way, or ignored a red flag, only to find out that it was actually something you didn't want, or worse, was a total disaster. Although rejection doesn't necessarily feel good, recognize that it could be a blessing in disguise. By surrendering to rejection, you are surrendering to the natural flow that will ensure you get the things that are meant for you in their due time.

CHAPTER 9
SAGITTARIUS: NOVEMBER 22–DECEMBER 21

With your big heart and even bigger appetite for life, you don't just grab life by the horns—you conquer it. Motivated by a deep-rooted sense of adventure, you eat, sleep, and breathe freedom. Whether it's freedom of thought, speech, religion, or movement, the ability to express yourself without impediment is crucial to your happiness. Unafraid to throw yourself into the unknown in your quest to learn and experience everything that the world has to offer, very little gets in your way when it comes to doing what you want, when you want. Problems arise when you can't be bothered to sit still long enough to follow through on a commitment, or when you get so stuck on an ideal that you shirk practicality and responsibility.

In this chapter, you'll discover ways that you can still be a free spirit without blowing off your responsibilities, while creating relationships with others that are nourishing and fulfilling.

THE FREE SPIRIT WITH THE WILD HEART

The jet-setter and the shaman. The intellectual and the goofball. There's a reason why your zodiac sign is linked to a creature that is half human and half beast; it's this duality that makes you both the wandering child and wise old soul that you are. This is also why people turn to you for your sage advice, entertaining stories, and thought-provoking conversation. Ruled by the planet Jupiter, also known as the god in charge in Roman mythology, your lifelong quest is to help the rest of us answer the big questions about life and our roles in it. This is why your sign is considered the teacher as well as the student. Despite your studies, you're not just interested in tackling the serious stuff. Represented by the warm, dynamic element of fire, and ruled by the planet associated with indulgence and abundance, you have a lighthearted nature that allows you to find the silver lining in just about any situation.

As the zodiac sign ruled by the planet associated with good fortune, you sometimes throw care to the wind in a way that leaves you disappointed when something doesn't pan out the way you hoped. When all is said and done, your lesson is to learn that it's the small working parts—including your close personal bonds and sticking to your word—that provide you with the most freedom. If you have a solid base to work from, you can go anywhere.

For all your enthusiasm and energy, problems emerge when you feel that your freedom is being threatened. This is when the more primal side of you appears, as you are ready to take off at a moment's notice, dropping your commitments rather than taking on the responsibility that lies before you. An idealist at heart, you can become so caught up in the promise of a dream come true, that you overlook the need to buckle down to actually turn that dream into something real. This results in numerous false starts and unfinished projects. In your relationships, this can also lead you to miss crucial red flags or seem noncommittal.

YOUR APPROACH TO LOVE

Speaking of your freedom, let's hope your date has got their bags packed, because it's going to take a lot to keep up with you when it comes to love. For you, love—like just about everything else in your life—is all about the adventure. Happily throwing your heart into the ring with the kind of confidence that might intimidate others, you have no trouble letting someone know that you're interested in them. As intelligent as you are funny, you win your crushes over with your no-holds-barred humor and brainy conversation. As with anything related to Jupiter, you like everything big and plenty, which includes your sexual appetite—and your well-endowed partners. But while you enjoy a healthy sexual appetite with those who may be physically stacked (or jacked), you're not only about sex. You need a significant other with brains as well as brawn, and an over-the-top sense of humor to boot.

Though you get pegged as someone with an inability to commit, because of your need for personal freedom, the truth is that you just need someone who has enough going on in their own lives and won't be turned off by your need to come and go as you please. You'll only consider a crush a keeper if they can broaden your mind and increase your frequent flyer miles too. The person who captures your heart long enough for you to see a future with them will be someone who encourages and admires your independent attitude and adventurous spirit. In fact, they'll be pretty adventurous too. As an outgoing fire sign, you never shy away from going after what you want. With an extra boost from the powers of color and scent, potential mates and dates will come running.

WOWING WITH COLOR

Standing out comes naturally to you, thanks to your larger-than-life personality. But did you know you can highlight your features even more with colors that showcase your wise soul, vibrant energy, and generous spirit? The following colors are tailored to your Sagittarian charm.

Indigo

Linked to the higher mind (Sagittarius's realm), including wisdom, spirituality, and integrity, indigo is a perfect power color for the shamanic sign you are. Wear this color when you want to channel confidence and a little magic too.

Purple

A dazzling combination of cool blue and fire-hot red, this is the go-to color for you, as it represents the mix of your fiery energy and your cool way of thinking. Go for the rich purple hues that represent wisdom and wealth when you want to feel like a million bucks. With your luck, you just might win some real cash too.

Turquoise

Representing ease of communication, good fortune, optimism, and mental clarity, turquoise is also the birthstone of your sign. It's considered to be a lucky and protective stone. Go for this color when you want to keep the vibe upbeat and attract positivity to you. Consider wearing turquoise jewelry when you need a little extra assurance.

SCENTS FOR POWER AND SEDUCTION

When it comes to seduction, why stop at color? You can also use specific scents to extend your unique brand of charisma even further. Thanks to your confidence and enthusiasm for life and love, it doesn't take much for you to start a fire. Still, you'll need a little fuel to keep the flames going. Spicy, resin, and herb-based fragrances are perfect for feeding your fire and burning your brightest. Seek out these notes when making your next head-turning potion.

Spicy

As a passionate fire sign, it only makes sense that spice-based fragrances are a perfect match for your peppery personality. When you want to feel in charge and in your element, go for fragrances or essential oils that contain these notes:

- Coriander
- Cumin
- Ginger

Resins

With their link to spirituality and healing, resins should be a mainstay in your boudoir when you want to give your partner (or *partners*) an out-of-body experience. You can also use them during those times when your spirit could use a little healin' of its own:

- Copal
- Frankincense
- Myrrh

Herbal

You're a free spirit known for your love of the outdoors and wide-open spaces. Fragrances that contain herbal notes inspire peace, tranquility, and an open heart. Go for fragrances or essential oils that feature these scents when you need a brief escape into nature:

- Blackberry Leaf
- Rosemary
- Sage
- Thyme

DAILY AFFIRMATIONS FOR LOVE

Now that you've got your new signature colors and tantalizing scents at the ready, it's time to plan your next "accidental" run-in with that new love interest, right? Not quite: there is still one more tool to keep on hand.

As an optimistic and philosophical Sagittarius, you also know the power that thoughts and words have when it comes to achieving happiness in love. Daily affirmations are a great tool in helping you stay the course toward the love life you want, ensuring that you keep the positive vibes flowing.

One of the things that makes you so irresistible is your openness with your heart and your affections. As a fearless fire sign, you greet love with a wild excitement and a wide-eyed sense of wonder—though, as courageous as you are, you easily get skittish when you feel that a partner is encroaching on your freedom. Because of this deep fear of being tied down, you can end up attracting significant others that are either too clingy or too flaky. On the flipside, when you do find someone you wouldn't mind sticking around for, you can become so idealistic about this person that you miss any signals that tell you they aren't *the one*. By the time the fog clears and your hope for improvement has worn thin, you're stuck feeling upset that you didn't see the warning signs in the first place. The following love affirmations are designed to help you gain clarity about what you want in love and to also get you thinking more about your current beliefs surrounding commitment and intimacy:

- I am capable of having a relationship that is stable and emotionally satisfying.
- I attract romantic partners that are honest and possess integrity.

- The right relationship for me is as passionate and sexually fulfilling as it is real, substantial, and deeply intimate.
- The perfect relationship for me is supportive of my independence, yet also teaches me the value of dedication and emotional intelligence.
- My partner is someone who I can travel with and who is always up for fun.
- My partner encourages my ideas, and values what I have to say. I can talk to them about anything and everything.
- The right partner for me is responsible and mature.

DEALING WITH HEARTBREAK AND BREAKUPS

Sometimes you may find yourself with a partner who isn't right for you or a relationship that has simply run its course. While this is a part of life, there are ways to get through heartbreak and remain optimistic about the future.

Considered the serial dater of the zodiac, you can get your heart broken—a lot. As a thrill-seeking fire sign with a thirst for life, you love fast, and you love hard. Seeing nothing but the best in your partner, you invest lots of time, energy, and faith in them, often believing more in them than they believe in themselves. It could be said that inside every Sagittarius is a life coach waiting to happen. Although, when you do find yourself life-coaching your romantic partners, it may be a cue to take a step back. This is because when you are this coach to your partner, they may become dependent on all this guidance, refusing to show initiative for themselves. They may also not share the same enthusiasm about being "coached" that you have. If a person is going to be successful, they have to also want it for themselves. In order to avoid these challenges in your relationship, you must give yourself the opportunity to truly get to know a person—paying attention to who they are, not who you're hoping they will be.

True to your positive nature, if and when you do find yourself facing heartbreak, you'll be able to find the teachable moment in this experience. Breakups show you what you do and don't need in your love life and where you may need to continue developing and growing.

Going through a breakup also means giving yourself space to experience your feelings. As a philosophical and wise Sagittarius, you often prefer to take the high road when it comes to an unpleasant situation. Though that may seem like a noble thing to do, it can actually rob you of your healing process. When dealing with heartbreak, it's necessary to face your shadows. Go ahead and ugly cry. Feel free to block your ex on every social media channel possible; don't force yourself to stay friends out of a need to save face or play it cool. Your healing is paramount, and those intense feelings you're having need to be released so that you can let them go. If you try to skip over them, they're going to keep coming back—most likely in the form of a new partner with the same lessons to teach you. Don't worry, these feelings will eventually pass so you can get back to being your happy-go-lucky self again.

HANDLING RELATIONSHIPS WITH FAMILY AND FRIENDS

Moving on to family: these relationships are often a tricky subject for Sagittarians, since home is not usually a place that you want to be tethered. In fact, your fears around being tethered to someone or something are not only a challenge in your romantic relationships, but also in the relationships that you share with your family. One the one hand, while you may feel like you need your family, you also dislike the idea of needing them, preferring your own space and the ability to come and go as you please.

Ultimately, when it comes to dealing with your family, your lesson is in how to navigate the delicate balance of preserving your freedom while recognizing that you are not an island. Deep human bonds are necessary to our well-being, and as frustrating as they can be sometimes, it's important to nourish and maintain those bonds—granted that they're healthy. Don't underestimate the power of your community.

You tend to feel the most comfortable in your relationships with friends, as you can enjoy more freedom by coming and going as you please. You may find yourself going days or weeks at a time without seeing or speaking to a friend, but still have the ability to reach out and catch up right where you left off. While any friendship can benefit from this freedom, it also makes you susceptible to accumulating friendships that lack substance, authenticity, and reciprocation. This is because you're either not sticking around long enough to establish deeper connections, or you're afraid of connecting with others. These friendships, while fun and easygoing, are often hard to count on when you may need them the most. To remedy this, you may need to be pickier about who you let into your circle, as well as more willing to extend yourself to those who you consider to be tried-and-true friends.

YOUR APPROACH TO CAREER

Your need for freedom doesn't stop at your personal life; you need it in your professional life too. While you don't necessarily have issues with holding down a steady job, you do need a job that either allows you to travel or work on your own schedule and provides you with the right amount of variety and room to grow. You certainly don't want a micromanaging boss breathing down your neck either, though you can sometimes end up with one by settling for jobs that you're not really invested in out of a lack of foresight, planning, or commitment to your career path. This is when you can find yourself stressed and unhappy or stuck in a loop of job-hopping.

When you do believe in what you do, you are one of the most dedicated and passionate professionals around, coming up with brilliant new ideas that positively impact and inspire others. Possessing the endearing goofiness, confidence, and goodwill to win people over, your influence on others extends far and wide. Plus, with your ability to throw caution to the wind, you don't mind taking a few risks to get where you want to go. It is no surprise that Sagittarians make the perfect life coaches, teachers, writers, and comedians.

Just don't jump up onto that stage yet. There are still a few things to consider when you prepare to take the next step toward success.

DAILY AFFIRMATIONS TO HELP YOU GET AHEAD

Daily affirmations are a great tool in helping you succeed in your professional life. These motivational phrases remind you of things to recall when taking on a new job, working toward a promotion, or reconsidering your current position. Through affirmations, you can really take the reins when it comes to achieving your professional goals.

You have no problem going after what you want, but you're not always discriminating about what you go after. This can lead to a lack of enthusiasm and irresponsibility down the line. The following affirmations will enable you to be more strategic and intentional about the opportunities you pursue:

- I am talented and capable. I put in the work necessary to hone and study my craft.
- I am dedicated to what I do, and I make sure I always do a thorough job.
- I am respected and welcomed for my ideas, voice, and point of view.
- My workplace is warm, welcoming, and conducive to productivity.

- I take my skills seriously and respect my worth.
- I recognize that time is money, and I respect my time and the time of others.
- The right job for me fills me with meaning and purpose.
- I know that I am deserving of professional opportunities that enable me to thrive.
- Whatever I set my sights on, I go after it with determination and follow through with my plans.
- I am focused and intentional with how I spend my time and energy; I only take on what I can do.

JOURNAL PROMPTS

In addition to these affirmations, it will also help you in pursuing your career goals to draw on past experiences. Use the following prompts to explore these situations, and discover how you can apply these situations to your present goals.

As a Sagittarius, you have a ton of ideas and enthusiasm when it comes to your career ambitions. However, you don't always possess the focus and follow-through needed to fulfill them. At the same time, you love the opportunity to learn and applying what you've learned toward your personal growth. The following questions will help you to glean the tendencies you may need to modify, as well as how you can better channel your energy toward your goals.

- Is there something you've started but have yet to finish? What would it take for you to complete it? What's one step you can take now toward this goal?
- What's the biggest problem you've had to solve to date? How did you solve it? What did you learn about yourself as a result?

- What do you find yourself complaining about? How can you turn those complaints into an opportunity?

DEALING WITH DISAPPOINTMENT

You've done everything you can, but still things aren't turning out the way you hoped. Unfortunately, disappointments are a part of the working world no matter who you are. But have no fear, there are ways to overcome these setbacks without losing your motivation.

As the forever optimist, disappointment is not something you tend to take well. Always setting your sights on your next big idea and usually finding a way to make things all work out, you are often quite jarred when your arrows don't hit your target as expected. At your best, you're able to find the meaning or nugget of wisdom in the experience, enabling you to dust yourself off and try again. However, in those instances where it feels harder to pick yourself back up, recognize that failure isn't a reflection of your abilities or your worth. You are not the sum total of your mistakes or failures; sometimes things don't pan out and it has nothing to do with you or how much effort you put in.

Additionally, there's a bit of a relationship between disappointment and desperation. While disappointment isn't always avoidable, it can highlight what happens when you want something so badly that you become desperate for it and how it feels when you don't get it. Being the fiery Sagittarius you are, you'll get angry first. You'll blame yourself next. Then you'll question your worth and use the experience to reinforce the fear that things will not work out.

If you find yourself on this side of the spectrum, take a moment to regain perspective. Challenge your beliefs. Know that desperation is the antithesis to abundance. Desperation is rooted in the belief that you must struggle to get what you want, because either no one will hand it to you, or you're undeserving of it. However, when you begin to recognize that what is meant for you will find its way to you, you can be excited for something without feeling like if you don't have it, you won't be able to be happy.

YOUR APPROACH TO WELLNESS

With your taste for everything in big heaping doses, one thing you have to be careful of is overdoing it. This goes for your schedule and foods or drinks that may be unhealthy for you. It's also important for you to learn the value of listening to your body and knowing when you need to pull back. That said, if you lead a relatively inactive lifestyle, listening to your body may mean getting it moving again. As a fire sign, you do need some level of physical exercise, as it helps you with staying motivated and focused. When it comes to your emotional well-being, it's also vital that you have outlets such as meditation and jogging to help you work through and release your more complex feelings.

MAKING YOUR HOME YOUR CASTLE

Before you race off, though, it's important to create a sanctuary that you can come home to for a little rest and rejuvenation. As a jet-setting traveler and restless spirit, you need a home base that provides you with a place to cool your jets and reconnect to your center. Linked to spirituality and religion, you can use the following items to cultivate a homegrown sanctuary that gives you the comfort and refreshment of a spiritual retreat:

- Incense like nag champa or frankincense and candles to create a space that feels sacred.

- Soft or natural lighting that's easy on the eyes and the nervous system.
- Soft, comfortable bedding to induce a more restful sleep. No sleeping on threadbare sheets or hard, boxy mattresses. Invest in your rest.
- Fresh water near your bedside to keep you hydrated through the night and refreshed upon waking.
- An inviting bathroom space, filled with lush bath-and-body products, where you can cleanse yourself of negative energy and unwind.
- Soothing and peaceful colors such as soft greens and blues (colors associated with water, the wide-open sky, and the cosmos) to provide a calming backdrop as well as a nod to your free spirit.
- Inspirational artwork, such as landscape photography, and framed mantras or motivational quotes.
- Soft music when you want to decompress, or noise-canceling earplugs to escape from the hustle and bustle of the world (roommates and family members included).

REKINDLING THE FIRE: TIPS FOR RECLAIMING YOUR SPARK

Sometimes you may need a little more help in bouncing back when all the hustle and bustle zaps your energy and enthusiasm. No worries, with a few simple techniques, you'll be back to your bubbly self in no time.

There is no worse feeling to a Sagittarius than feeling stuck or as though your wings have been clipped. If you've been in this position before, you know how upsetting, disorienting, and at times dull that feeling can be. Fortunately, there are simple ways to get your spark back.

Find Something to Celebrate

As the party animal of the zodiac, you may not need explanation here. However, every so often when you're at the point where your arrows aren't landing where you want them to, or you're in one of those crunch zones where it's all work and no play, this is when you can find yourself running short on your usual abundance of optimism. When this happens, take it as a sign that you need to let loose and have some fun.

Move Your Hips

One of the body parts that Sagittarius is linked to are the hips. In eastern traditions, hip movements can also be used to align the Root and Sacral chakras—energy points within the body near the lower spine, pelvis, and hips that connect us to emotional well-being, material wealth, creativity, and sensuality. For a Sagittarius, stiffness in the hips can manifest as issues with money and self-worth, pessimism, and a lack of inspiration. If you're experiencing any of these setbacks, try putting on some of your favorite music and letting your hips do the talking. As you move, imagine you're pulling the things you want toward you. You'll be surprised at how quickly they show up.

Grab Your Bow and Arrow

Sometimes when you've hit a rut, there's nothing else to do but what you do best: let your arrows fly toward something new and see what sticks. You don't need to have a specific target. All you need to do is allow yourself to be curious and to commit to your desire. Figure out what resonates with you right now at this moment. You'd be surprised at the obstacles you can get past, the resources you can find, and the opportunities you can uncover when you give those seeds of desire permission to flourish.

Have a Make-Out Session

If there's one thing that the element of fire is connected to, it's raw passion—including the sexy kind. There's a reason that Sagittarians have a reputation of, uh, you know...getting around. That fiery zest for life and lusty appetite translate to the bedroom too. Sometimes there's nothing like getting sweaty with a hottie to reignite your spark. It's said that kissing boosts your self-esteem, immune system, and mood—so go get 'em, Sagittarius!

Challenge Something You Believe

Your beliefs mean a lot to who you are. In astrology, Sagittarius is associated with philosophy and religion. Yet, trouble can arise when you become dogmatic about what you believe, refusing to question or challenge any opinion. Your beliefs can quickly become a prison for you, robbing you from seeing the bigger picture or opening yourself up to something new. As the zodiac sign connected to the quest for truth, an old belief can keep you bound to one way of thinking or experiencing life. So, the next time you find yourself feeling stuck in a rut, ask yourself whether something you believe is keeping you from growing. Stress can also be a factor in stunting your growth, which is why it is essential to have a few tools on hand to help you keep cool under pressure.

KEEPING COOL UNDER FIRE: TIPS FOR RELIEVING STRESS

You're one of the zodiac's feel-good signs, which means you rarely let things get you down, stress you out, or stop you from having fun. However, there are going to be times when you won't be able to slap a smile across your face and keep things moving. Sometimes life is overwhelming and frustrating and messy. The following are a few tricks for handling these situations head-on while still coming out on top.

Feel It Out

It's no secret why people crave touch: it can stir up the libido, increase intimacy, and foster relaxation. The next time you feel anxious, burned out, or cranky, try running your fingers through a lush piece of fabric, lying down on a crisp pair of sheets on a freshly made bed, or oiling up your skin with coconut oil infused with rose oil or patchouli. Instead of gobbling down your food, savor it slowly. The goal is to slow down and flood your body with pleasure.

Make Ritual a Practice

With your active lifestyle and aversion to boredom, it isn't hard for you to jam-pack your schedule with one too many activities. Before you know it, you're feeling overwhelmed and stressed out. This means you'll either blow off a responsibility, struggle with procrastination, or burn yourself out trying to juggle everything. By creating a space in your schedule for a soothing daily ritual like yoga, gardening, or cooking, you are able to slow down and become more focused and intentional with how you spend your time. The best rituals are those that bring you a moment of solitude and a way to tune in and reconnect with yourself. It shouldn't involve TV or anything that can be considered a distraction.

Bathe

The element of water in astrology is considered to be healing and cleansing and is linked to emotional fulfillment. In daily life, it is easy to take water for granted, but it can be one of the most powerful tools at your disposal when it comes to stress relief and your well-being. Although you have a reputation as a happy-go-lucky, optimistic zodiac sign, you can accumulate lots of mental and emotional energy that can fester as negative thinking and fear. Bathing helps to clear out your emotional cache and balance out your Sagittarian fire. Envision yourself releasing whatever may be bothering you into the water and down the drain, especially things that you have no control over or that happened in the past.

Honor the Shadows

This is one of the most important, albeit challenging, steps that you can take when you're feeling anxious or stressed out. It's important because it acknowledges that you don't have to always be the shiny, happy person that you or others may expect you to be. It means that you are embracing the full spectrum of yourself, not just the pretty pieces. One way to do this is by acknowledging how you feel. Make room for it. Honor it. Don't try to skip over it or press forward. Channel the energy into something cathartic like an intense workout or a form of art. Writing a good angry poem or song can do wonders with getting those feelings out.

CHAPTER 10
CAPRICORN: DECEMBER 22–JANUARY 19

A trailblazer of impeccable character and refined taste, you know the value of rolling up your sleeves and getting your hands dirty to get stuff done. Not only do you know how to handle your business, but you do it so well that others often come to you for your expertise and advice, trusting you to show them how to handle their business too. Although you're a true leader by birthright, your stripes and accolades have been hard won thanks to your willingness to dig in and do the hard work. However, as mature and responsible as you are, you can still run into your share of trouble, over-working and undernourishing yourself and also alienating those who care about you in your quest for wealth, security, and status.

This chapter is dedicated to helping you focus on what matters beyond your bank account and professional credits, like your physical health and well-being and your relationships with friends, family, and significant others.

BOSS-LEVEL STATUS

Reserved and meticulous, you don't expend your energy on anyone or anything unless you know it's worth it. Ruled by Saturn, the planet linked to responsibility, rules, and achievement, you approach the world with a no-nonsense strategy and a realistic outlook. For you, time is money and you don't like wasting either. However, you're no Scrooge; you are always ready and willing to offer friends and family a helping hand, even at a moment's notice. Whether you're providing someone with financial advice or lending your time and skills to helping out a friend in need, when folks call on you, you are ready to help.

Blessed with the ability to build things from scratch (like a *Fortune* 500 company), your mission in life is to create a solid foundation by which you can leave behind a legacy. You teach the rest of us how to turn our ideas and passions into something tangible like a well-funded money market account. Not one to sit around waiting for anything to be handed to you, you have the kind of ambition that helps you to leave the competition well behind. As the zodiac sign connected to status, awards, and recognition, you have no trouble with putting in the long, painstaking hours to sharpen your skills and get ahead. Your dedication to success is what makes you both envied and admired among your peers. For you it's work first, rewards later, and it's no surprise that many Capricorns—including Kate Moss, Stephen Hawking, and Betty White—have built iconic careers based on this kind of work ethic.

However, things start to get a bit sticky when your preoccupation with rules and responsibility prevents you from being open to change, or able to go with the flow. As someone with an innate understanding of how quickly things can go wrong and fall apart, you pride yourself on keeping the chaos away through your preparedness and cautious nature. Although your ability to keep things in check is one of your gifts, you can paralyze yourself with a fear of losing your security, bringing out the control freak in you. Ultimately, one of the biggest lessons that you must learn is how to operate from a place of security from within—how to stay centered and grounded in an ever-changing world. This doesn't mean that material wealth and security are a bad thing, but over-identifying with it can put you in a risky place where you are willing to do everything in your power to keep it. Your goal is to establish your own internal compass that supports the courage and peace of mind that comes from being true to yourself and your values—no matter your salary. This compass will also guide you through other aspects of your life, including love.

YOUR APPROACH TO LOVE

As someone who prefers action over talk, your affections don't come easy, nor do they come cheap The person who can claim your heart is one who is willing to dedicate themselves to the work it takes to earn your trust and respect, as well as keep you happy. And it doesn't stop there. Once in a relationship, you expect a partner to maintain that same level of commitment because you're more than happy to do the same. Thanks to your understanding of the amount of patience and care that goes into maintaining a relationship, you're not the one to give up on a romance at the first sign of trouble. Longing to be one half of a power couple, you usually go for the ambitious and successful types like yourself (à la Kate Middleton and husband Prince William). Nevertheless, you don't mind pitching in and helping your partner reach success if you see enough evidence of drive and effort on their part (like Michelle Obama and husband Barack Obama). At the same time, you also need a compassionate partner who softens the world's sharp edges on your behalf. As someone who prides yourself on being a realist, you can be prone to cynical or pessimistic thinking. Because of this, you need a little love and kindness in your life to balance out the harshness of reality. A loving partner will brighten your doorstep with joy and romance. In terms of sexual satisfaction, you need someone as lusty and kinky as you are.

And speaking of lusty, you'll want to have a few extra tricks up your sleeve when you are seducing a potential partner. These tools include power colors and tantalizing scents. The admirers are going to be knocking down your door.

WOWING WITH COLOR

It's important to feel sexy in your skin. After all, love begins with the love you have for yourself. The following colors highlight your earthy, sensual, yet no-nonsense sign, leaving you with a sense of power and dazzling confidence. Incorporate these colors into your wardrobe to put the world on notice: when it comes to getting what you want in life and in love, you mean business.

Black

A power color, black is the go-to for you because of its association with authority, status, and depth. From the boardroom to the bedroom, wearing black will leave an impression that your admirers will never forget.

Blue

Darker shades of blue, like navy or cobalt, represent stability, integrity, and confidence. As a capable and competent babe, you have no trouble showing the world that you're on your game. Wear these shades when you want to give folks a little reminder.

Gray

Gray is a very chic and sophisticated color, matching your very chic and sophisticated style. It is also linked to the Capricorn qualities of maturity and wisdom. Considered a neutral, gray will allow you to make a statement without saying too much.

SCENTS FOR POWER AND SEDUCTION

In addition to your new power colors, scents are a great tool in ramping up your confidence and magnetism. Powerful, sensual, and unforgettable—you need fragrances that highlight these gifts. Look to scents that are based on warm, woody notes as well as floral and herbal fragrances. These fragrances will highlight your earthy nature.

Woody

It may take you a little while to warm up to a partner, but once your engines have been revved, there's no stopping you. Go for fragrances and essential oils that feature these earthy and erotic notes when your engines could use a jump start:

- Cedar
- Cottonwood
- Mahogany
- Pine

Floral

Timeless and chic, floral fragrances are a nod to your understated elegance and polished style. These notes are strong without being overpowering and linger well after you're gone—much like the Capricorn legacy. Go for these scents when you want to make a lasting impression or get back to being the boss that you are:

- Night-Blooming Cereus
- Orange Blossom
- White Tobacco

Herbal

Healing and soothing, these notes are the perfect go-to after a long, stressful day at work. You can use herbal fragrances to de-stress and relax, which also makes you more open and receptive to love and romance:

- Eucalyptus
- Green Pepper
- Wheat
- Wormwood

DAILY AFFIRMATIONS FOR LOVE

You've got your power colors and seductive scents ready to go, but before you set your sights on that special someone, there is a little more planning to do. As a sign that *loves* a plan, you'll especially love using affirmations to set a plan for your love life. These daily motivators will also keep a negative outlook about love at bay. As a loyal partner, you have no qualms about giving 110 percent in a relationship. In fact, your need for security can result in sticking with a relationship long past its expiration date. Considering yourself to be a practical person, you may forgo your emotional needs for the sake of financial security or a partner who looks good on paper. On the flipside, you may also attract people who are overly clingy and dependent, due to your need to be in control. Essentially, you need a partner who can feed your heart as well as your 401(k) plan. The following affirmations are designed to help you attract that person into your life while reminding you that you are deserving:

- My perfect match is equally dedicated to our partnership.
- The right person for me is reliable, responsible, and wants to build a future with me.
- My partner fills up my heart as well as my bank account.
- I honor my need for tenderness and sexual compatibility.

- My partner encourages me to be open to change and brings positive new experiences into my life.
- My partner is financially thriving and is generous with their resources.
- The right relationship for me provides me with security and growth.
- When I'm with my partner, I can truly be myself.

DEALING WITH HEARTBREAK AND BREAKUPS

Being a pragmatist, you know that love isn't always forever. Still, dealing with a breakup can be upsetting. Fortunately, there are ways to push through without losing all hope for love.

As a Capricorn, you invest so much in your relationships, that between the sting of failure and hurt feelings, it can be hard to let go and throw all your hard work down the drain. Since you do invest so much, you have no qualms about exhausting all your options in trying to fix any issues that arise in a relationship. The trouble here is that not only does your partner have to be equally invested in repairing the issue, but in your effort to fix what's wrong, you may be forcing something that's not meant to be. You have to know when to cut your losses. Additionally, just because something didn't work out doesn't mean that it was a waste of time. Relationships are not only about the experiences, but also the lessons you learn about yourself and what you do and don't need in a relationship going forward.

If you find yourself dealing with a breakup, recognize that this is an opportunity for you to grow, becoming stronger and wiser than you were before. As uncomfortable as dealing with your more complex feelings may be, know that it's okay to feel sad or even cry. While you're used to doing things alone, you shouldn't go through a heartbreak alone. Now is the time when you should be leaning on your friends and family. Also, be mindful of the energy you are putting out to your ex. While it's perfectly natural to be consumed with thoughts about them, recognize that placing too much focus on wanting to hurt them back or make them pay prolongs their presence in your life. As someone who also prides yourself on how loyal you are to those you love, you expect that same loyalty in return. This means that you may also see a breakup as a betrayal if your partner was the one who initiated it. The best thing you can do is focus on moving on and healing your wounds. Celebrate the gift of having you all to yourself; you're an amazing person to be with. Friends and family will also attest to this fact.

HANDLING RELATIONSHIPS WITH FAMILY AND FRIENDS

No stranger to responsibility and willing to come to the aid of a family member in need (especially on a financial level), it's no surprise why your family looks to you as the glue that holds everything together. While you may get a certain amount of pleasure (and even praise) from coming to the rescue of those you love, an imbalance can occur when you position yourself as the one your family always runs to for assistance, instead of solving problems on their own. Giving so much and receiving little in return, this unequal family dynamic will leave you feeling resentful and emotionally depleted. However, you should consider that it may be difficult for your family to give back to you, because you may refuse help in your time of need out of a fear of appearing weak or needy. Your lesson here is to allow yourself to be more vulnerable. Start asking for help when you need it, reminding yourself that it is not a sign of weakness.

On the other hand, you may be straining your relationships by making it hard for others to come to you for help, doling out lectures or tsk-tsking them when they do. If you do find yourself in this scenario, tenderness can go a long way in turning things around. Work on being less judgmental and more compassionate when someone comes to you in their time of need.

Your friendships share a similar theme as your family dynamics, as you're often the rock that others come to depend on. One thing that you need to watch out for is overstepping your boundaries when it comes to the lives of your friends. While you may have a genuine desire to help, you can find yourself coming on a little too strong, taking on a parental role or attempting to play therapist with a friend when all they might have wanted was a sympathetic ear. Overall, when it comes to your close relationships, Cap, try a little tenderness.

YOUR APPROACH TO CAREER

Now that you've made it through the mushy stuff, it's time to move on to a topic you really can appreciate: your career. Capricorn is *the* sign of success. This is why you've earned the reputation of being a hardworking, business-savvy money magnet. With no-nonsense Saturn on your side, you pursue your career goals with shrewd thinking and a dogged determination. Thanks to natural-born leadership skills that stem from your self-starting nature and need to create and uphold the rules, you are drawn to roles in government and administration, law enforcement, and business management. Since your sign is also interested in building things from scratch, entrepreneurship, engineering, and architecture are also great fields for you.

Jobs and working environments that lack clear goals, objectives, or structure will drive you nuts—unless there's an opportunity for you to jump in and take the reins in order to whip things into shape. Many a Capricorn have made history by starting small and climbing through the ranks to the top of their field, due to their ability to see the things in need of improvement and know just how to fix them. Opt for jobs that fulfill your need for productivity and that also provide you with opportunities for mobility and recognition.

DAILY AFFIRMATIONS TO HELP YOU GET AHEAD

While you're busy climbing to the top, there are some encouraging affirmations that will help you along the way. These motivational phrases not only ensure that you are putting out the positive vibes that will draw opportunities to you, but also remind you of things to recall when taking on a new job, working toward a promotion, or reconsidering your current position.

You don't bother with big-picture ideas unless you have a plan of action to actually make those ideas happen—fairy tales certainly aren't your thing. You have no problem with calling a spade a spade and taking a no-nonsense approach to getting what you want. These qualities are certainly admirable, especially when it comes to reaching your goals. Yet, realistic thinking can easily turn into pessimism. The following affirmations will help you to focus positively on what you *do* want, as opposed to the things you're unhappy with or don't want:

- I am determined and capable. I can knock down any challenge that stands in my way.
- I am resourceful. I turn my mistakes into wins.
- I welcome the opportunity for change and positive growth.
- I make time for myself and my needs. I recognize when I need to push and when I need to take a break.
- I make time for the people who love me; I succeed with their love and support.
- I am valued for my expertise, my leadership, and my innovative ideas. I am confident in what I bring to the table.

- I attract professional relationships that are fulfilling and financially rewarding.
- The right job for me offers me financial security and enjoyment.
- I feel good about the professional decisions I make. I know that I am always choosing what's best for me.

JOURNAL PROMPTS

As a Capricorn, you need to be able to actually apply everything you are learning to real life. Prompting questions are a great way to get you thinking proactively about how to use your knowledge to create the professional life you desire.

Being the zodiac sign linked to success and responsibility, it can be hard to take risks with your career by making professional decisions that veer off a conventional path. While stability and financial security are important, there are times when showing up solely for a paycheck won't be as rewarding as it should be. The following journal prompts are designed to help you step out of your comfort zone to truly flourish in the working world:

- What do you think you could achieve if you were to let your heart lead the way forward?
- When it comes to your "failures," in what ways could you stand to embrace your flaws?
- Spend some time tracking your thoughts. Make note of any time you think negatively or criticize yourself about something. Replace that thought with something self-affirming. How do you feel each time you do this? Do you notice a positive shift in how you think or feel?

DEALING WITH DISAPPOINTMENT

There are times when something is easier said than done, and you are met with a bump in the road. Luckily, there are ways that you can handle a professional setback without losing your confidence. True to your self-motivating and enterprising nature, no one pushes themselves as hard as you do or expects so much of themselves. Where others may fall short on patience, skill, or preparation, you go the extra mile to make sure that whatever you do turns into a success. One reason for this is that as a critical sign, you often believe that you're undeserving of success, which motivates you to push yourself all that much harder. This is why when you fall short of a goal, it can feel like a devastating blow. As a result, you spiral down a path of negative thinking and harsh self-criticism, thinking that every mistake you've made since the distant past has led you here.

Being a Capricorn also means that you care a lot about what others think of you. Thus, you invest a lot in your public image, making career decisions that include obtaining certifications and specialized degrees that will bulk up your resume and offer recognition. With you investing so much in your public image and accolades, getting past the disappointment of losing out on a potential client or promotion can throw you off your game. The good news is that Saturn, your patron saint, has bestowed you with an unmatched self-resilience and determination that will enable you to prevail. Nevertheless, you don't always acknowledge these gifts. The beauty of astrology is recognizing that you already possess the solutions to the challenges that life throws at you. Dealing with a professional setback is easier when you acknowledge your gifts. Still, don't feel you have to immediately snap back from a disappointment. Although you pride yourself on your stoicism, allowing yourself to mourn a professional loss can be helpful. For one thing, you're releasing the feelings rather than holding on to them, which helps you to move on faster. You are also channeling a direct line to your intuition, inspiring mental clarity through the exploration of your feelings. In other words, don't be afraid to delve inward in order to reconnect to your center.

Activities that are self-affirming and meditative will also help you to turn down the volume of your self-doubt and leave you open to success in not just your career, but also your personal well-being.

YOUR APPROACH TO WELLNESS

There's no doubt about how hard you work. In fact, your office is more than likely your second home. However, for all the time and energy that you put into your business plans and boardroom meetings, it's important that you play (and relax) just as hard. Otherwise, you can find yourself dealing with skin rashes, allergies, body aches, or depression as a result of taking on too much. Make sure that your living space is set up to recharge your batteries for that next conference call.

MAKING YOUR HOME YOUR CASTLE

Being the busy professional that you are, you're either barely home or working from home, which leaves you with little time for cleaning or upkeep. You need a home base that allows you to quickly recharge your batteries so you can get back to work. Here are a few essential items for creating a perfect space just for you:

- Warm, vivid colors, like red or orange, to energize you and stimulate positive energy. In Eastern traditions, red is also associated with abundance and financial security. As a sign linked to financial wealth, these colors will help you feel like you're always in alignment with the abundance you seek.

- A minimalist or low-maintenance home décor theme that appeals to your functional needs as well as your crisp, clean aesthetic. This may mean chucking rugs that clutter the room or having multipurpose furniture, like a coffee table that also doubles as a storage unit.
- Organizational items that can help to keep your zone free of clutter. This means less stuff for you to trip over or sort through as you're headed out the door.
- Materials for DIY projects around the house, which can spark creativity and help you channel restlessness or stave off boredom.
- A dedicated work area to support your late-night work and brainstorming sessions. Keep work out of your bedroom and bed for better sleep.
- Industrial home-design accents or pieces that make a statement while speaking to your earthy, pioneering personality. This includes exposed light bulbs and an apothecary cabinet, which can also double as useful storage space.
- Candles or artwork that bring in the element of fire to stimulate passion, drive, and an openness to new experiences.

STAYING GROUNDED: TIPS TO KEEP YOUR FOOTING

With a firm home foundation to work from, you're (almost) ready for anything. You will also need a few tools for staying grounded when life throws you a curveball. While self-care does require discipline and hard work, your goal is to work on being kinder to yourself. The following exercises in self-love will help you keep (or regain) your footing when things don't go as expected.

Honor Your Creativity

You often get a bad rap for being inflexible, but the truth is that you become rigid only when you allow yourself to be motivated by fear instead of determination. You are actually quite creative and innovative, possessing the ingenuity, ambition, and dedication to turn initial sparks of inspiration into complete projects. Honoring your creativity may mean giving yourself a consistent outlet like painting or dancing. Allotting time to this activity will help you to tame unproductive mental chatter and find clarity while also renewing your energy and enthusiasm.

Sign Up for a Class

As an earth sign, you thrive on productivity and turning ideas into something tangible. You also know the value of practicing your craft to improve your skills. As enterprising as you are, however, you can fall prey to rigid thinking and stagnation out of a fear of losing your security. Pushing yourself to be open to new things will help you to ignite your inspiration and get back out into the world to do what you do so well. As a bonus, you will also be picking up a marketable skill.

Make Pleasure a Priority

As an earth sign, it's vital for you to be connected to your physical body in a sensual and pleasurable way. Self-pleasure; body work such as massage or Reiki; and indulging in other tactile delights, like sleeping on plush bed linens or wearing satin pajamas, will help you to make this connection. Even if you have to pencil some of these activities into your busy schedule, make them a priority. When you are in a space of regularly feeling good, you attract more good things to you.

Take Care of Your Skin

In astrology, one part of the body that Capricorn is in charge of is the skin, which is why when you're feeling off-balance, one of the first telltale signs is the state of your skin. Barring any serious medical issues, skin that's too dry, patchy, or prone to blemishes is often a result of stress hormones being released into the body. Astrologically speaking, the skin is what helps hold the body together and provides the first barrier of protection against the elements, germs, and other potential dangers. Taking care of your skin can be as simple as making sure that it's properly hydrated and well moisturized. This simple act of self-care can also alleviate stress, so break out some rich coconut oil or shea butter!

TENDING THE EARTH: TIPS FOR RELIEVING STRESS

In addition to caring for your skin, there are a number of easy ways to tackle stress—or avoid it altogether. Relaxed and collected: a stress-free Capricorn is a happy Capricorn. Use the following techniques to reach that happiness.

Practice Gratitude

When you consciously choose to focus on the good things, whether it's finding a dollar on the sidewalk or getting a phone call from one of your favorite people, you'll be amazed at how quickly the good things add up. In fact, when you make the act of gratitude a regular part of your day, you start to pull more good things toward you. Try coming up with a list of at least five good things that have happened to you today. The things on your list can be as big or as small as you like. If you can come up with five, try coming up with ten. Can you make it to fifteen total things? Making this a regular activity will remind you that things aren't as bad as they may temporarily seem.

Talk about What You're Feeling

As a stoic Capricorn, you might be comfortable providing an ear for friends and family, while refusing to lean on others in your own times of need. You take great pride in your ability to pull yourself up by your own bootstraps. This means that you tend to bottle up your feelings until they are pushed more and more toward depression or nervous tension. By talking with someone about how you feel (therapy is always a good option), you can lighten the load on your shoulders and find a sense of peace. Get into the habit of opening up to others, maybe by letting them know up front how you need them to listen. For example, do you just want to vent? Or do you need some words of encouragement? Let people know how they can show up for you, and they will, which will make it easier for you to lean on them.

Don't Skip Meals

In a nonstop world, work is valued so much that it is easy to let personal health fall to the wayside. As a Capricorn, you're no stranger to putting in long hours at work, often opting to work through your lunch or to skip meals entirely. This puts you in a place where you are functioning in a condition of depletion and imbalance. Stay in the wavelength of abundance and well-being by making time to eat, and eat well.

Cultivate a Spiritual Practice

Saturn, your ruling planet, represents reality and the cold hard facts. This makes you prone to excessive worry, pessimism, and depression. One way that you can reduce stress and stave off the blues is by creating a spiritual practice. Having a sacred space and a dedicated time to convene with the Spirit, nature, yourself, or a combination of all three, gives you a nourishing emotional and spiritual well to drink from whenever you are in need of replenishment. This way, when things start going haywire, you are able to maintain your calm, optimism, and well-being. You can start your practice by creating an altar adorned with pictures, flowers, candles, and other items that speak to you on an emotional level. Use this altar as your space to meditate, pray, recite mantras, or to simply breathe. Whatever way you do choose to spend this sacred time, it should be something that uplifts, heals, and empowers you.

CHAPTER 11
AQUARIUS: JANUARY 20–FEBRUARY 18

Known as the rebel child of the zodiac, you don't follow trends, you set them. Your ideas are fresh, innovative, and two steps ahead of everyone else. Fearlessly going against the grain, you strive to create a world where the differences between people are not only accepted but celebrated too. Quirky and independent, you have little patience for being held down by norms or rules that trample on your self-expression or personal freedom. This is why when it's time to shake up the status quo and stick it to *The Man*, you're the first one out on the front lines, striving to be the change that you want to see in the world. Despite your gifts, you can encounter challenges when you swing wildly between extremes out of a need to stir things up and maintain your personal freedom.

In this chapter, you'll learn how to find a place of balance and equilibrium in your relationships, career aspirations, and personal health. You'll also discover ways to channel your unconventional gifts into everything you do, including attracting a potential partner, finding the perfect job, and overcoming whatever obstacles life throws your way.

THE REBEL WITH A CAUSE

Ruled by Saturn, you have a fixation on the rules, tearing them down in favor of a better system—especially when the preexisting rules only benefit a small fraction of society. This is where your secondary ruler Uranus comes in. In astrology, it is Uranus's job to break the rules and societal norms. Although you fancy yourself a person of the future, you can find countless other Aquarians in history who dedicated their lives (and at times sacrificed their safety) to create a better world. These include Susan B. Anthony, Jackie Robinson, and Audre Lorde, whose activism centered around causes that included equality for women, equality for African Americans, and equality for the LGBTQ community. As an air sign, not a moment goes by that you aren't coming up with your next idea. Your sharp intellect makes you and others born under your sign some of the most innovative thinkers around. Thanks to your genuine care for others, many of your ideas are geared toward supporting the collective. Your mission is to teach the rest of the world how to work together as a community while still making room for one another's individuality.

Due to your unique outlook and need to be independent, you may at some point have dealt with being the odd duck of your community. A major theme in your life is honoring your individuality regardless of how unaccepting others may be. When imbalanced, you tend to struggle with either people-pleasing at the expense of your own needs or becoming so nonconformist that you alienate yourself from others. Essentially, your biggest lesson is learning how to express yourself in a way that honors your individuality without trampling on the individuality of others. One way to do this is by recognizing that your beliefs about things aren't necessarily the correct or only beliefs. Honoring your individuality will go a long way in succeeding in all aspects of your life, including love.

YOUR APPROACH TO LOVE

Not one for jealous rages or sticky-sweet emotional displays, you consider yourself to be a cool-as-a-cucumber, equal-opportunity partner who expects the same from your love interests. Eschewing convention, cookie-cutter romance is not your shtick. You would much rather be single than worry about picking out the perfect china for your country-club wedding. Besides, a commitment ceremony on Mars sounds much more romantic. While friends and family might not understand your long-distance love affair with a goat herder in Turkey, it makes all the sense in the world to you, and you're just fine with that. At your best, you provide your partners with that *je ne sais quoi* factor: the indefinable thing that they can't get anywhere else. Of course, they better be able to offer you the same.

WOWING WITH COLOR

Speaking of that *je ne sais quoi* factor, did you know you can play it up even more by using the power of color? As an innovative and unconventional zodiac sign, it doesn't take much for you to stand out. Still that doesn't mean that you couldn't use a few tools to complement what you've already got going on, especially if it means taking your magnetism and your confidence up a few notches. What follows are colors that are specific to Aquarius and that represent your cool and intellectual nature.

Pale Blue

Pale shades of blue work for you as an air sign, because blue is representative of communication and clarity. You can go with a monochromatic look to play up the power angle in a gender-bending business suit, or a mix of pale blue tones to show off just how chill you are.

Multicolored Patterns

While this might seem like an option better suited to your flashy opposite, Leo, multicolored patterns enable you to command attention and separate yourself from everyone else. If you're really feeling bold, consider using a super-vibrant color combo like pink and orange to make your presence known.

Silver

As cool as you are, you don't need a ton of help looking the part. Still, silver (especially metallic accents) will help you to stand out among the crowd while looking your best.

Dressed in your one-of-a-kind duds, you are ready to take the world by storm—almost. Color is just one way to stimulate the senses—did you know you can also use specific scents to draw the admirers to your door? One who loves having options, you'll be happy to hear that there are quite a few fragrances out there that are ready to help you seduce that new love interest.

SCENTS FOR POWER AND SEDUCTION

Avant-garde. Bold. Edgy. These are just a few words to describe your matchless personality. When it comes to your signature scents, you need fragrances that highlight your eclectic tastes. Read on to discover the perfect scents to complement your edgy, one-of-a-kind personality. Your admirers don't stand a chance.

Woody

These notes make up fragrances that are considered unisex, which is music to Aquarius ears, as you are not about being locked into one category. Go for fragrances with these notes when you're in the mood to switch things up a bit. Since these scents also have a calming quality, you can also use them to soothe frazzled nerves and open yourself up to love:

- Cedar
- Lichen
- Sandalwood
- Vetiver

Aromatic

Fresh and distinctive much like you, aromatic notes help you make a statement while playing it cool. Fragrances and essential oils that feature these scents will also calm the body and the mind—which can be what you need as an on-the-go air sign:

- Fennel
- Lemon Balm
- Marjoram
- Mint

Spicy

You love to keep things interesting, and as such there's never a dull moment with you. That's why you need a signature fragrance that celebrates your unique, high-spirited approach to life. Go for fragrances or essential oils that contain these notes:

- Cassia
- Star Anise
- Pimento
- Tonka Bean

You've got your signature colors and seductive scents, but before you fire up your online profile to meet that special someone, there is one more item to add to your arsenal...

DAILY AFFIRMATIONS FOR LOVE

Daily affirmations are another great tool for attracting the love life that you want. Affirmations ensure that you put out positive vibes while also serving as a reminder of what you are and are not looking for in a partner.

As much as you celebrate your personal freedom you can be incredibly self-conscious deep down about fully being yourself—specifically in an intimate relationship. Because you may be used to being an outcast of sorts, you wonder if someone can truly accept you for you. As a result, you can end up attracting people who trigger your insecurities by attempting to change you. Your fear of vulnerability and being yourself can also attract self-centered partners who treat you and your heart with carelessness. The following affirmations will help you turn your love life around by recognizing the accepting, loving relationship that you deserve.

- My partner loves me and accepts me as I am.
- My partner understands me and gets my unique point of view.
- When I am with my partner, I am able to let my guard down without reservation.
- Friendship, communication, and true partnership are the hallmarks of my relationship.
- My partner is protective of my heart and treats me with care.
- The right person for me is genuine, fun-loving, and always up to try something new.
- My partner brings balance and positive energy to my life.

DEALING WITH HEARTBREAK AND BREAKUPS

Even with these positive affirmations by your side, breakups are often still a part of love. Don't fret—there are a few ways you can handle these heartbreaks and still come out on top.

Though you have a hard time letting others in, once you do let them in, they're in forever. As a fixed sign (meaning enduring and long-standing) you thrive on security. Also, as an air sign (a sign linked to friendship), you thrive on strong bonds. Despite this, a fear of losing your independence can drive you to sabotage the relationship by pretending to be unfazed by any conflicts or hurt feelings. In trying to play your hand so cool, you give your partner the idea that you're not as invested in the relationship as they are. To remedy this, you must learn to honor your emotions and express them clearly. This can be a scary and uncomfortable thing to do, but vulnerability creates a bridge between you and your partner, whereas fear can drive you apart.

While a main coping mechanism for air signs is to rush off and try to meet someone new, your heart needs time to heal, and it's okay for you to admit this. In fact, admitting that you feel terrible is the first step toward bouncing back. Good ways to release these feelings are by breaking out your journal or allowing yourself space to cry. Tears can be quite cleansing for the soul. If you need a shoulder to cry on, you can always look to a friend. As you know—or will learn—friends and family members will be a great asset in many parts of your life.

HANDLING RELATIONSHIPS WITH FAMILY AND FRIENDS

Even though you need your independence, your connection to your family is your lifeblood. Family is your foundation, your safe haven, and your calm in the eye of the storm called life. Still, problems with your family relationships may arise if an emphasis has been placed on material wealth and security. As someone who tends to create your own lane, you may be drawn to careers and life choices that your family may find unconventional and may be less than enthusiastic about. As such, you could feel like an outcast or the black sheep of the family, thereby reinforcing your fears about being an outsider. Your biggest lesson in your family relationships will be determining your own barometer by which you live and knowing this measure might mean a lack of approval from your family members. While you certainly don't have to shut anyone out, you may need to choose standing your ground over trying to keep the peace.

Regarding friendships, you have friends from all kinds of areas of life (thanks to your varied interests, ability to make friends with ease, and diverse life experiences). As independent and free-spirited as you are, you don't need to keep up with your friends on a regular basis, as you share the kind of bond that makes it easy for you to pick up where you left off—whether the last time you saw them was yesterday or last year.

However, because of your friendly nature and can-do attitude, you may find yourself attracting friends who need a life coach or a spiritual adviser more than anything (air signs like you struggle with spreading themselves too thin and people-pleasing). This means that people will take advantage of your kindness. If you do find yourself in the company of people who make you feel more drained than happy, it is time to take a look at the friendship. Additionally, you might also be met with the challenge of trying to keep everyone happy all the time. If you try to attend everyone's events, and donate to all their fundraisers, and make yourself available to everyone else whenever they ask for your attention, you're going to run yourself ragged. At the same time, you'll be left wondering why no one does the same for you. To avoid these problems, get more comfortable with saying no, and start working on building relationships that are more reciprocal. For example, is it time to end a friendship that feels one-sided? Can you be vulnerable enough for your friends to come to your rescue?

YOUR APPROACH TO CAREER

Now that love and relationships have been covered, let's talk money! As the zodiac's resident rule breaker, you gravitate to jobs and professions that provide you the opportunity to leave your own stamp on the world. Careers that you may be drawn to include political activism, government administration, social services, and the nonprofit field. One to clash with your superiors because of your need to question authority and to ask the tough questions, you are also drawn to jobs that allow you to work alone or unsupervised. Careers like this include start-up founder, app developer, scientist, graphic designer, or even indie filmmaker.

Your needing to do your own thing also makes you a bit reluctant to follow rules and listen to authority. Why limit yourself to one person's beliefs when you can add your own thoughts to the mix? However, rules are sometimes necessary to getting a job done well and on time, so you will need to moderate your rebellious side. This will also help in team situations where camaraderie is a key component of the company culture and enables you to be an effective member of the team.

Due to your taste for the weird and unconventional, you might also pursue careers that are off the beaten path, like hypnotherapy or, *ahem*, astrology. Whatever you choose to do for a living, you pursue it with an almost obsessive determination, refusing to take no for an answer, or to quit before you've reached your goal.

DAILY AFFIRMATIONS TO HELP YOU GET AHEAD

Quitting definitely won't be an option with a few motivational mottos up your sleeve. Using affirmations attracts the exciting, engaging career or job advancements that you want while encouraging positivity—even when your career goals aren't turning out as you had hoped.

As someone who struggles with being fully accepted by others, you can become easily discouraged if you feel like you have to play office politics or like you don't fit in with the culture. These affirmations are designed to help remind you that your uniqueness is an asset rather than a setback and that you have the intelligence, resourcefulness, and determination to achieve your goals.

- I am headstrong and determined; I never give up on what I believe in.
- I respect my need to pursue a career that I love. I attract paid and professional opportunities that fulfill me.
- I recognize when it's time to move on to a job or career that's better suited for me, and I take the steps to make it happen.
- I am innovative, intelligent, and committed to improving the world. I am a valuable asset.
- I respect my skills and the investment that I've made in my training and expertise. I say yes to opportunities that compensate me accordingly.
- I am respected by the people I work with, and I respect them too.
- I recognize when it's appropriate to question authority and when I may need to trust the process.
- I have a job that offers me healthy challenges and engages my brain; no two days are the same.
- I recognize when a job negatively affects my health and when it's time to move on.
- The right job for me makes me feel like I am making a difference in the lives of others.

JOURNAL PROMPTS

You can move things a step further by using prompting questions to explore how you can take some of the challenges you may be facing in your career and turn them into opportunities for growth. Uranus, your planetary ruler, often gets a lot of the credit for your zodiac sign's traits in astrology. As the planet that's associated with upheaval and sudden change, this is why many people attribute your sign as being in need of constant change. However, the other planet in charge of your sign (Saturn) is not so enthused about sudden changes. Saturn likes rules and things being in their place. This means that as an Aquarius, you are prone to Saturn's pessimistic thinking and fear of change. The following journal prompts are geared toward helping you work through these challenges so that you can truly thrive in your position.

- Where do you think you may be resistant to change? In what ways can you be more welcoming of change?
- Have you ever had an idea that you wished you could turn into something real? If you had the chance, how would you do it?
- Have you ever lost out on an opportunity? How were you able to bounce back from that loss?

DEALING WITH DISAPPOINTMENT

When you have done your best and your professional plans *still* don't work out—what do you do? Deep breaths, Aquarius, there are easy ways to deal with these setbacks like a boss. For all your independence, you still crave security, even if it's the security of being able to come and go as you please. This means that you'll often apply a ton of focus and determination to accomplish your goals, refusing to give up along the way. There's a reason why so many activists are Aquarians. Because of your desire to improve the lives of others, you'll do whatever it takes to succeed. However, when it comes to dealing with something like disappointment, it can be hard for you to accept a setback. In other words, for you, failure is not an option.

In order to move past these disappointments, you have to be willing to relinquish your control. In doing so, you're challenging yourself to overcome your tendency to internalize failure as a reflection of yourself and your capabilities.

The second key to dealing with a disappointment is recognizing that a failure doesn't mean you are letting others down. As an Aquarius, you have a deep desire to help others, and although wanting to change the world is a noble goal, it's also a lofty one. By keeping your ambitions and your goals realistic, you can set more obtainable ones. This will also help you to attain overall well-being.

YOUR APPROACH TO WELLNESS

As an air sign, you love being thrust into the action, learning new things, soaking up information online, and talking and connecting with a myriad of people throughout the day. Still, with your eclectic personality and spontaneous schedule, you are prone to anxiety, insomnia, and a scattered, absent-minded energy when you overextend yourself.

MAKING YOUR HOME YOUR CASTLE

To avoid frying your circuits, you need a living space that provides you with an element of structure and a grounding energy. The following are a few essential items for achieving a stable, relaxing space. These items will also ensure that your home is as unique as you are:

- Wood or copper accents, as well as raw crystals or stones (like a salt lamp or rose quartz), to bring a grounding, tranquil energy into your home.
- Pastels, neutrals, or earth tones to evoke a quiet and relaxing vibe—namely in the bedroom and anywhere else you're likely to unwind.
- Plush linens, pillows, and carpeting to create a cozy and lived-in feel.
- Scented candles that contain soothing scents like vanilla or lavender. These accents also add to the cozy aesthetic of your living space.

- Designated areas for your mail, keys, and phone so that you can not only avoid clutter, but also be able to remember where you last put something down.
- Greenery, like low-maintenance houseplants, succulents, or a small herb garden, to promote abundance and good health.
- A well-stocked fridge and munchies on hand so you can refuel frequently and save money by not eating out.

GETTING FRESH AIR: TIPS FOR HELPING YOU FEEL RENEWED

Represented by double waves of electricity traveling through the air, you are prone to an overabundance of nervous tension. One reason for this is because Aquarius is in charge of the circulatory system. When you're off-balance, spread too thin, or stressed out, you can become restless, anxious, and struggle with insomnia. Luckily, there are ways that you can combat stress and feel better.

What happens when air stops moving or circulating? Things get pretty stagnant—suffocating, even. When you're at that point when you feel like you're stuck, you might feel like you're suffocating too. Following are some ways to get fresh air—ways you can hit the reset button and feel renewed.

Put Your Ideas Onstage

Witty and creative, you have no shortage of ideas. Boost your confidence by sharing these ideas with the world! Perhaps this is your moment to pitch that article you've always wanted to write, or to do a live reading of the collection of poems you've been working on, or launch that photography website you've been meaning to put out. When you take the time to share your voice with the world, not only are you performing an act of self-love, but you're also helping to make the world a better place.

Flex Your Inner Robot

With your scientific mind and your innovative way of thinking, sometimes delving deep into galaxies or alternate futures is just the thing you need for a reboot. You can do this by getting lost in the latest sci-fi film or book, trying out a new gaming experience (hello, virtual reality), or doing a bit of cosplay at the next sci-fi convention of your choice. Not only is it a lot of fun, but it will also spark your creativity and your ability to think outside the box in ways that can benefit you in other areas of your life (like your professional life). You might even feel inspired to come up with tech or stories of your own.

Go on a Cultural Dig

As a curious air sign, you get a kick out of learning new things. Why not turn the chance to learn something new into an opportunity to explore new cultures as well? You can do so by traveling, signing up for a workshop or museum crawl, or by befriending someone from a different background. The goal is to wake up your brain while having fun too.

Reinvent Yourself

Isn't it time for a new hair color—shocking pink or electric purple, perhaps? How about bright yellow nails to go with your bright yellow raincoat? You don't have to spend tons of cash—unless you want to. You can easily find your next statement piece at a thrift shop or experiment with the makeup you already have. You don't have to stick to beauty either. You can find a new job, consider relocating, or work on mastering time management. Whatever you choose, it should be something you can accomplish with minimal stress.

Flirt

When you're feeling run down, romance is one of the first things to go. Tap into your flirty side to reinvigorate your love life—or just to have a little fun. The act of flirting gives you a boost of confidence and puts you back in a playful mood. And guess what? When you're feeling good, it attracts good things to you.

KEEPING IT EASY-BREEZY: TIPS FOR RELIEVING STRESS

Part of feeling good will be combatting the stresses that seem to pop up at every turn. Fortunately, there are a few simple ways to tackle these tensions head-on and still come out strong.

As an Aquarius, you are prone to anxiety and nervous tension, especially when you've spread yourself too thin. Following are a few exercises for avoiding those frazzled nerves and providing yourself with adequate outlets for self-expression.

Stay Hydrated

As an air sign with an active lifestyle, you should keep your body well-nourished and hydrated, keeping your energy levels up and your body working like a well-oiled machine. In fact, if you take a moment to tune into your body, you can even feel how your mood or your energy shifts when you've gone too long without food or water. When you starve your body of what it needs by skipping meals or waiting too long to hydrate, it can throw your system into panic mode, which elicits nervous tension.

Protect Your Energy

Although you're a people person, you can be quite susceptible to taking on the negative energy of others. That said, pay careful attention to who you give your attention to, even if it's a well-meaning yet complaining neighbor or an angry coworker. You don't owe anyone your time or attention.

Pay Attention to How You Feel

While tapping into your feelings might not be your forte, there's something to be said for giving yourself space to feel them. Not only do feelings have a direct line to intuition, but they can also give you clues as to when you may be in need of some extra rest or a change of pace. When you try to ignore how you feel, you can find the emotions spilling out in inappropriate ways, like a panic attack on the subway platform. Start paying more attention to how you feel, and practice tapping into what your body needs.

Honor Your Vulnerability

Don't be afraid to be vulnerable. No need to go through a tough or stressful time alone! Learn how to ask for help when you need it and be open to receiving it. You might just find that you have more people in your corner that are ready and willing to assist you than you realize. Aquarius is the sign of friendship and community, after all.

CHAPTER 12
PISCES: FEBRUARY 19–MARCH 20

A natural enchantress, there's nothing that you can't have with one of your bright-eyed smiles and a dose of your loving attention. But you're no phony: your genuine kindheartedness is just one of the things that makes you a rare gem in a world of people who often aren't what they seem. It's also why people are drawn to you in droves, hoping to get a piece of your magic. As a sensitive and compassionate soul, you help to heal the world through love. Blessed with spot-on intuition, you can pick up on things before they happen, making it possible for you to stay one step ahead of the game. However, things can quickly go off-balance for you when you avoid trusting your intuition or exercising your boundaries.

In this chapter, you'll learn what you can do bring the balance back to your life, including tips on how to beat stress and use your magic to ramp up your love life and your career.

THE MERMAID AND THE MAGICIAN

Though you're made up of flesh and bones, you are often compared to beings of magic and mysticism. This is because your planetary rulers, Jupiter and Neptune, bestow on you a mysterious allure, borderline psychic intuition, and the ability to make your dreams happen. As a water sign, you are most concerned with emotional and spiritual healing, including bridging the gap between the emotional and spiritual realms. During this quest, you teach the rest of the world lessons about compassion, forgiveness, faith, and love in all forms.

While many people peg you as being soft and easily pushed over, the fact of the matter is that while the rest of the world hides from their wounds and tries to cover up their vulnerability, you courageously love and accept others, despite the risk of being hurt. Your ability to see and feel another's suffering while providing exactly what they need to heal, makes you a magician in your own right. Meanwhile, your natural sweet charm has you raking in the admirers with little effort.

With your intuitive insight, you have a wisdom and knowing about you that transcends time and the physical world, which at times can have you feeling a bit disconnected from this earthly plane, even when it comes to your physical body. Other times, you are so plugged into the physical realm, that you are in need of a quiet escape to stay sane. Part of staying sane also means setting and maintaining boundaries. Without healthy boundaries, you are vulnerable to giving too much of yourself or absorbing too much (specifically negative emotions) from others. Either way, you are left feeling drained on a mind, body, and soul level. Ultimately, what you must guard against is sacrificing yourself and your happiness on behalf of the needs of others. This skill will translate to many parts of your life, including family relationships and love.

YOUR APPROACH TO LOVE

You're bewitching, with a compassionate nature and an uncanny sixth sense. You get off (and get your partners off too) by creating relationships that blur space, time, and the physical world. Your presence and attention are so addictive that your partners may find it hard to avoid your spell, which means you're never short of admirers. Needing romance like the rest of us need air, you crave connections at a soul-deep level. You want to feel inseparable from your partner, and you'll do what it takes to create that bond. In the next section, you'll discover new ways to turn up your confidence and your charm to attract a love worthy enough of your devotion.

WOWING WITH COLOR

As the zodiac sign associated with fantasy and dreams, you know how to pull out all the stops and the charms to woo a crush. Still, you never have to try too hard, as you understand that a big part of seduction is establishing an emotional connection with the object of your affection. But that doesn't mean you don't like to titillate others with your sensuality. Through the use of your power colors, you can become more self-assured while wowing your admirers.

Blue
Reminiscent of the ocean or the lush tropics, sea blues—especially blue-greens—inspire refreshment, renewal, and a sense of calm. Make this your go-to when you need a bit of confidence-boosting juice or you want to feel rejuvenated.

Lavender
Delicate and soothing, lavender is the perfect color for laid-back vibes and also for leaving an impression without being overpowering. Go for this

color when you want to maintain your inner chill while looking cool at the same time.

Rose

Pink hues, like rose and blush, speak to the romantic in you. Go for these soft shades of pink when you want to play up your sweet allure. Wearing fabrics like silk, satin, or linen in shades of rose or pink will also add a romantic touch to your wardrobe. You'll have your admirers eating out of your hand in no time.

SCENTS FOR POWER AND SEDUCTION

And speaking of eating out of your hand, you can make yourself even more delicious by using the power of scent. True, you hardly need help with attracting potential mates and dates. But even a magician like you should have a few extra tricks up your sleeve.

Floral

Soft, fresh, and hard to resist, you won't find anything better than floral scents to capture the essence of Pisces. Wear perfumes or essential oils that feature these fragrant flowers to highlight the enchanting nurturer within:

- Jasmine
- Lilac
- Sweet Pea
- Tuberose

Fruity

Refreshing and bubbly like you, fruity fragrances or essential oils boost your mood—and your popularity with your admirers. Go for scents in this fragrance family when you're feeling flirty or could use a pick-me-up:

- Currant
- Kiwi
- Pineapple
- Watermelon

Sweet

Sugar, spice, and everything nice is exactly what you are made of. Use these notes as your guideline for discovering or creating your go-to scents, especially during those times when you're feeling a bit carnal and want to serve yourself up as a tasty treat:

- Almond
- Brown Sugar
- Vanilla
- Whipped Cream

DAILY AFFIRMATIONS FOR LOVE

A romantic at heart, love is never too far from your mind. So, before you head out that door in your best blue dress and lilac perfume, there is one more item to consider. Through daily affirmations, you can use the power of your thoughts to attract the love you want. These motivational words ensure that you put out positive vibes while also serving as a reminder of what you do and do not need in a romantic relationship.

As a sensitive water sign with a heart as big as an ocean, you have tons of love to offer a partner and rarely shy away from opening your heart. You could even say that, as a Pisces, you *love* love. There's something about those first inklings of romance, coupled with heady anticipation, that sets your heart aflutter. Before you know it, you're giving your new love the keys to your apartment and wondering why it's been a week since you have seen them. This is by no means a knock on you. The rest of the world would be lucky to have the bravery that you have to open their heart as readily and fully as you do. However, because of your giving and loving nature, it's easy for less-than-savory people to be drawn to you, as they mistake your kindness for something they can take advantage of. The following affirmations are designed to help you attract the reciprocal relationships that you deserve and expel the unbalanced relationships that you don't.

- I am capable and worthy of being loved as I want to be loved.
- I am discerning with my heart and my tastes. The perfect partner for me demonstrates their love through words and actions.
- I recognize when I am letting my idealism get in the way of what's really in front of me. I love with my eyes open and make my choices accordingly.
- The perfect partner for me is trustworthy, thoughtful, and romantic. I feel comfortable trusting this person with my heart.
- My partner is my rock—stable, loyal, and supportive.
- When I am in my partner's company, I feel completely and totally adored.
- The perfect relationship for me feels heaven-sent. I have found my soul mate.
- I attract romantic partners that possess integrity and are of solid character.
- The sexual chemistry between my partner and me is filled with tenderness, love, and passion.

DEALING WITH HEARTBREAK AND BREAKUPS

No matter how much you put into your relationships, heartbreak and breakups can still be an inevitable part of life. But not to worry—there are ways to make sure a heartbreak doesn't hinder your ability to seek out and find love in the future.

Intuitive and emotional, you feel everything at a soul-deep level, including breakups. Unfortunately, when you don't push yourself to be discerning about the kind of partners that you give your heart to, it will end up broken. While it doesn't take you long to fall for someone, getting over a significant other may take months, or longer. As an emotional water sign, you not only feel things very deeply (like love) but you also spend a lot of time thinking about and ruminating over the past and what could have been. Thus, you may have a hard time with letting your ex slip completely out of your life, prolonging the breakup and healing phase. This is why one of the first things you should do after a breakup is cut off all contact with your ex. You should also let go of their belongings, which may be taking up space in your home, wash or throw out the sheets that the two of you slept on, and even burn a stick of sage to smudge your ex's energy out of your home. You have to cover all your bases: mind, body, and soul.

You may also benefit from a ritual breakup bath. As a water sign, bathing is one of the most powerful tools that you have when it comes to healing and releasing pain. Consider having the bath during a Full Moon, as Full Moons represent endings. As you bathe, imagine that you are washing your ex out of your system for good.

HANDLING RELATIONSHIPS WITH FAMILY AND FRIENDS

As you know, romance isn't the only form of love: there are family and friend relationships to take care of as well. While you usually share a close bond with your family, one thing that can ruffle your fins is the feeling that your family relationships aren't as emotionally supportive as you would like them to be. This can occur when you take on the reputation as being the emotional one in your family, lending an ear or shoulder to everyone else and not having anyone to lean on in return.

The key to successful relationships with your family is in honoring your need for emotional support while also recognizing that, although you're deeply in touch with your feelings, you have to be able to speak up to family members and say exactly how you feel instead of trying to avoid a conflict. By the same token, you may also need to ask questions for clarity to make sure your understanding of a situation isn't being clouded by your emotions.

When it comes to your friendships, you are kind and amicable to the people around you, but it takes you a while to develop true and lasting friendships. A lot of the time, it takes learning how to be discerning with the kinds of people you consider to be friends. Since you're helpful and see the best in others, you may not always immediately recognize when someone is not really the friend that they claim to be. To avoid being taken advantage of by flaky or disingenuous types, you need to allow people to prove themselves to you through their actions, not just their words. The people you call friends should be people who you can lean on and derive strength from in your time of need.

Your task with friendships is to also learn how to establish valuable connections with people who can help you on a professional level. While you tend to get turned off by the idea of networking, because it gives you the feeling of coming off as a sleazy salesperson, it doesn't hurt for you to have a few friends in your corner who can help you to succeed. Ultimately, the goal of networking is to establish genuine and thoughtful connections. The genuine connections that you create can not only lead to tried-and-true friends that assist you in your time of need but also to career opportunities. And as you know, networking is everything in the professional world.

YOUR APPROACH TO CAREER

Creative and soulful, you are drawn to fields where you can express your deep well of creativity. Pisces, like Rihanna, Lupita Nyong'o, and Jon Bon Jovi, are attracted to creative fields like music, beauty, and entertainment because of their penchant for creating rich fantasies—fantasies that provide a form of healing and escape. As an intuitive, empathic sign, you are also drawn to fields where you can heal others on a physical, emotional, or spiritual level, such as nursing, counseling, or spiritual advising. Because of your introverted personality, you thrive in environments where you either work with few people or have the ability to leave work at work where it belongs, as you need frequent solitude to recharge your batteries from all the energy that you give to others. You also thrive in careers where you can set your own hours and even take on more than one role to satisfy your varied interests. You do need to be mindful of taking menial or easy jobs that don't challenge you or push you to grow, as well as jobs that consistently underpay you.

DAILY AFFIRMATIONS TO HELP YOU GET AHEAD

Through a few affirmations, you can ensure that you are never underpaid again. Daily affirmations are a great tool in helping you stay the course toward your dreams, reminding you of your magical powers—powers that will manifest the kind of career that you want.

You've got the power to dream big, and the kind of intuition and magnetism to draw things to you with minimal effort. However, sometimes a lack of follow-through and impractical thinking can stop you in your tracks before you even get started. The following affirmations will help you focus your magnetic power on attracting what you want while keeping you on track.

- I am talented and capable. I put in the work necessary to hone my craft.
- I am dedicated to what I do, and I make sure I always do a thorough job.
- I am respected and welcomed for my ideas, voice, and point of view.
- My workplace is warm, welcoming, and conducive to productivity.
- I take my skills seriously and respect my worth.
- I recognize that time is money, and I respect my time and the time of others.
- The right job for me fills me with meaning and purpose.
- I know that I am deserving of professional opportunities that enable me to thrive.
- Whatever I set my sights on, I go after it with determination and follow through with my plans.
- The right opportunities for me provide me with opportunity for growth and expand my knowledge through rewarding experiences.

JOURNAL PROMPTS

You can push these affirmations even further through the use of prompting questions. These journal-writing exercises will help you identify and overcome whatever obstacles come your way. While you're no slouch when it comes to going after what you want in life, there are times when some extra discipline or follow-through will make all the difference in how quickly you can achieve your goals. The following prompts will encourage you to explore your desires on a deeper level, motivating you to see your goals through to completion.

- In what ways are you confident in your worth? When it comes to your income, in what ways can you stand to be more confident when pursuing what you're worth?
- Have you ever taken a job that you were excited about at first but felt disappointed in later? What would you have done differently?
- How do you define discipline? In what ways can you stand to be more disciplined in your career or job search?

DEALING WITH DISAPPOINTMENT

Still, regardless of your efforts, setbacks are bound to occur once in a while on your path to success. So, what happens when it feels like you've run out of magic and nothing seems to be going your way on the job front? Not to worry—there are a few ways to deal with disappointments without losing your confidence.

As a Pisces, you are a dreamer. It's one of the things that makes you so creative, and gives you the ability to deliver an experience, service, or product that makes others feel like you created it just for them. However, there are times when you can dream so big that it can seem like an impossible undertaking once you get started. You may get so overwhelmed that you decide to quit altogether, leading to feelings of great disappointment.

Nevertheless, should you find yourself facing disappointment, first things first: let yourself off the hook. Beating yourself up about a setback will only make you feel worse, not to mention afraid to try again. What you *can* do is learn from the experience. Take note of where things may have gone wrong or became overwhelming. Since hindsight is twenty-twenty, ask yourself what you would have done differently if you had the chance. Then, determine the best way for you to proceed with your plans in the future. This may mean that you need to scale back on your approach or be more realistic and detailed with your planning or research.

Before you go back to the drawing board, though, make sure you're feeling good and ready to take on the world. This includes taking care of yourself. Yes, Pisces—you deserve tender love and care too!

YOUR APPROACH TO WELLNESS

As a water sign, you are prone to losing your steam and getting emotionally burned out. Since the element of water is more responsive or reactive than active in astrology, you have to make sure you have ways to keep yourself motivated and focused so you don't grow stagnant. At the same time, you also have to make sure you have tools to replenish your cup and keep it full. This includes creating a living space that supports productivity.

MAKING YOUR HOME YOUR CASTLE

While you may like to take things slowly on the outside world, your home is where the action really takes place. This is your global headquarters for everything under the sun besides sleeping and eating. This is where you love, dream, create, and have fun. You need a home base that can provide you with all the bells and whistles for whatever strikes your mood. Here are a few key items to get you started:

- Cool sea colors such as shades of blue and green as well as seashell tones to cultivate a calming oceanic vibe. Blue and green can also help promote mental clarity.

- Fresh flowers, especially in shades of white or pink, to invoke romance, purity, and a dreamy fairy-tale vibe.
- Accents that have sentimental value.
- Video games, a collection of books, and an entertainment system on hand that can provide you with an escape whenever you need it.
- Music instruments, drawing tools, and other creative elements that you can play around with when the mood strikes. Working with these items can boost your creativity and clear your head.
- Cozy blankets for your nap sessions. Refrain from bringing your gadgets and electronics to bed, as they can disturb your sleep.
- A designated area (like an altar) for meditation or spiritual practice, to assist you with clearing your mind and replenishing your spirit.

GETTING FRESH WATER: TIPS FOR FINDING YOUR FLOW

Because of your heightened sensitivity, you need to be careful of emotionally expending yourself into exhaustion by absorbing other people's feelings and energies on a regular basis. Otherwise, you might find yourself leaning on alcohol or other mood-altering substances for relief.

You're in that place where you feel zapped. You feel drained—washed-up, like you've lost your magic. Don't fear, Pisces, dear—with a few simple exercises, you will be back to creating that magic that makes you unique.

Don't Force It

There are times when no matter how hard you try to make something work, it just doesn't. As a water sign, there are times when you just need to go with the flow, tuning into your body and your mood and taking a cue from both. Sometimes walking away from a project or situation to give yourself time to chill is exactly what you need to get back on track. So, if you find yourself feeling stuck or off-kilter, it's okay to rest and relax. Take a bath, have a chat with a friend, or take a nap. Go with the ebb and flow; you'll find yourself exactly where you need to be.

Allow Yourself to Be Spoiled

As the zodiac sign linked to healing, selflessness, and sacrifice, you give much of yourself to the world and those around you. The trouble with this is that you can end up giving to others until there's nothing left to give to yourself. While your compassion and sensitivity is admirable, you need to make sure that you allow some of that energy you give away to be returned to you. A great way to do this is through a ritual. Whether it's getting pampered at a nail salon or having your friend or significant other treat you to something nice, get into the habit of being spoiled—even if you have to be vocal about letting others know what you want. Ask and you will receive.

Find Yourself a Muse

What inspires you? It's important as the most artistic sign of the zodiac to have things from which you can derive inspiration. Sometimes going through a creative dry spell means that you need to invite more play and spontaneity in your life to find new inspiration. It could also mean paying closer attention to your intuition. How can you invite something new and inspiring into your life today? You just might be kick-starting a juicy creation.

Mind Your Energy

As the zodiac sign that lives beyond borders, you can find it hard to keep from absorbing the energies of others. One minute you can be feeling good and ready to conquer the day, then *boom*: an interaction with a grumpy coworker or too much time spent around a drama-prone friend has you feeling completely drained and off your game. This is why it's helpful to guard your time and energy as fiercely as you can. Even if you must share space with people you would much rather not be around, you can set up an invisible barrier around you to block out their bad vibes. Start by taking a deep breath and clearing your mind. Imagine that you're enveloped in a bubble of white light. Feel that white light around you. You can also repeat a simple mantra like, "I am only attracting positive vibes today," or, "Peace and protection," as you imagine that light being a barrier for you.

Get Grounded

The thing about water is that it needs a place to settle, otherwise it just keeps on going and never stops. If you're at a place where you feel like you can't catch up to yourself, developing a practice for grounding can help. Basically, you're using your body to help you feel more rooted to the earth so that you can operate from a calm and clear place. One exercise for getting grounded is standing barefoot and slowing down your breathing with deep, intentional breaths. Imagine that your feet are like roots of a tree, trying to push down and find their way into the earth's core. Tune in to how your legs and feet feel. You should feel anchored. You can also do this in a seated position, using your tailbone as the source of the roots.

RIDING THE WAVE: TIPS FOR RELIEVING STRESS

Now that you've got your flow back, you'll need a few techniques to keep things from spilling over. As an adaptable Pisces, sticking to a schedule isn't something that comes easy to you. You need to have freedom to move about as you please. Yet, stress can set in when you put off important responsibilities until the last minute or you overextend yourself, taking on unnecessary obligations. The following are tips on how you can combat stress and shake those anxious or nervous feelings.

Work Up Your Confidence

When was the last time you did something that made you feel like a boss? Was it nailing a project at work? Finishing the story you wrote? Paying off your bills and having some extra cash left over? While you don't have to aim for big-ticket items like, say, getting a promotion (unless you want to), try to do something on a regular basis that feels self-affirming. It can be anything from getting through a difficult rep at the gym to teaching yourself a new skill. Whatever you choose to do should feel challenging yet fun and serve as a reminder that you're the sh*t.

Get Productive

Oftentimes, stress can be a result of feeling like either you have too much to do or that you're not doing enough. If you find yourself feeling like you aren't doing enough, don't wait for things to pile up on you. Try breaking up your task list into smaller, less daunting tasks. You can also space something out over the course of a few days. The act of tackling things one by one alleviates stress by giving you the feeling of accomplishment. Just make sure you follow through, so you can free your time up for something much better.

Talk about How You Feel

Even though you are super intuitive to how others feel, not everyone is. This means that if something is weighing on you, let others know how you feel, rather than waiting for them to notice. Sometimes the very act of stating out loud what bothers or scares you is crucial to reclaiming your power over it. Don't suffer in silence.

Be a Little Selfish

How many times have you agreed to do something for someone out of guilt or a feeling of obligation? How many times have you felt like you've done so much for others and as a result are unable to do much for yourself?

It's time to put the word *no* back into your vocabulary and take back your time. You don't have to be cold or rude about it, but sometimes saying something like, "I would love to, but I'm busy that day," or, "Thanks for thinking of me, but I'll have to pass this time," is all that stands between you and the things that you actually want to do. In other words, don't be afraid to be a bit selfish.

ABOUT THE AUTHOR

Mecca Woods is a New York City–based astrologer and writer who works to help others create a life they truly want using their natural-born gifts. Her writing and horoscopes have appeared in *Essence, Bustle, xoNecole,* and *PopSugar*. When she isn't writing, Mecca teaches astrology classes around the city on love, compatibility, and personal development. Her most important job is being a mom to her awesome Aries daughter. You can find Mecca at MyLifeCreated.com.